Sartre and Surrealism

Studies in the Fine Arts: Art Theory

Donald B. Kuspit
Chairman, Department of Art
State University of New York at Stony Brook

Kenneth S. Friedman, Ph.D.
Consulting Editor

Other Titles in This Series

Sartre and Surrealism

by
William Plank

umi
RESEARCH PRESS

Produced and distributed by
UMI Research Press
an imprint of
University Microfilms International
Ann Arbor, Michigan 48106

A revision of the author's thesis,
University of Washington, 1972

Library of Congress Cataloging in Publication Data

Plank, William.   •
    Sartre and surrealism.

    (Studies in fine arts : Art Theory ; no. 2)
    "Revision of the author's thesis, University of
Washington, 1972."
    Bibliography: p.
    Includes index.
    1. Sartre, Jean Paul, 1905-   —Criticism and
interpretation. 2. Surrealism—France.   I. Title. II. Series:
Studies in fine arts : Avant-garde ; no. 14.
PQ2637.A82Z815 1981   848'.91409   81-431
ISBN 0-8357-1175-7   AACR1

. . . le merveilleux est toujours beau . . .
—Breton, Premier manifeste

Le réel n'est jamais beau.
—Sartre, L'Imaginaire

Contents

Introduction

The confrontation of any two systems of thought will almost inevitably produce points of contact without, however, proving any real relationship between them. For this reason, this study is not a point by point comparison of Sartre's philosophy with surrealism, a lengthy task, but rather an investigation of Sartre insofar as he was concerned, explicitly or implicitly, with surrealist ideas and techniques. It will be seen then that this is a study basically of Sartre—but of surrealism only insofar as it has been necessary to discuss it to analyze Sartre's objections. In treating these objections I have not meant to defend surrealism, but merely to clarify surrealist intentions in the face of Sartre's frankly unsympathetic attitude.

It has not been necessary to ask "What is existentialism," for we are working with one man's attitudes and writings. But "What is surrealism" might be a more appropriate question: Is it Breton? Or the early period of intransigeance and excommunication? Or the later, more mellow period? There is some difficulty in a rigorous definition of surrealism because of its evolution over several decades and its manifestations in its various members. Sartre recognized this problem but was not bothered by it. I have, in general, been content to accept Sartre's definitions, since it is with his ideas that we are working, and have not tried to justify any particular surrealist position by appealing to its later evolution. Sartre did not undertake any complete evaluation of the movement in its evolution, and probably had no interest in doing so.

Surrealism and existentialism are perhaps the two major movements in twentieth-century France: the first getting an impetus in some way from its rejection of the attitudes that produced World War I; and the second, particularly in Sartre, developing as a way of coping with the problems of the occupation and the personal and social irresponsibility that made World War II possible. Both are movements aiming at fulfilling the human totality, and the problems they face are similar: What is a man's position in relation to the external world? What is the role of art and literature in life? What is one's reaction to absurdity and despair? How does one make the transition from the individual to the social? What is one's position in relation to Marxism and the Communist party?

The period between the two wars, years we might call the Golden Age of surrealism, saw Sartre grow from adolescence to manhood, between the ages of 12 and 34. It is quite natural that a young intellectual should take into consideration one of the major movements of that time; that it should show up in his own work, whether in satire or in a preoccupation with common problems. The two main works of prose fiction we will consider, *Le Mur* and *La Nausée*, are both from that period. The later novels of *Les Chemins de la liberté* do not show the same preoccupation and seem to be a transition to the later socially-oriented Sartre, as we will see at the end of Part I.

The study will be divided into two parts: first, the consideration of Sartre as anti-surrealist, and, second, the affinities of Sartre with surrealism. We will in general be restricted to the interwar years or to shortly after World War II, and to Sartre's prose fiction and essays, since his theatre is fairly traditional in form and presentation. This is not to say that surrealism died in 1939—it has had an indelible mark on modern literature and art. Maurice Blanchot wrote in 1949, "Il n'y a plus d'école, mais un état d'esprit subsiste. Personne n'appartient plus à ce mouvement mais tout le monde sait qu'il aurait pu en faire partie."[1]

For reasons of clarity and neatness of presentation I would have preferred to keep Part I (Sartre as anti-surrealist) distinct from Part II (his affinities with surrealism). However, as we shall see, these aspects are curiously interwoven in some of the fiction, particularly in "Erostrate," and in Sartre's objections to surrealism in *Qu'est-ce que la littérature?*, particularly in relation to Marxism and social action. I have therefore found it sometimes inadvisable, even impossible, to separate them. When Sartre used some particular aspect of surrealism, the *objet surréaliste* for example, to apply to several of his objections, I have followed his organization.

Sartre as Anti-Surrealist

The Demolition of the Subconscious

At the root of most of Sartre's objections was the surrealist belief that part of human reality lies hidden, unknown, and for a large part unknowable. Not only is it out of man's control, but he would be wrong to try to force an intellectual structure on that fecund source of the marvelous, on that part of himself which connected him to biological continuity, to magic, mystery, and nondifferentiation. Acceptance of that other world, the unconscious (or subconscious), seriously affects a philosophy based on consciousness, a lucid subjectivity, freedom, and a consequent responsibility.

André Breton's often quoted definition of surrealism[1] is based on the assumption that the subconscious mind exists; and automatic writing, more generally automatism, the major technique of the surrealist, further assumes that a certain truth lies in the subconscious. If we can overcome the deleterious effect of the rational faculties, this subconscious will express itself, destroying, in effect, the opposition between conscious and subconscious and producing a more complete human reality.

In the second chapter of *L'Etre et le Néant* where he discussed bad faith, the lie to oneself, Sartre pretty well dismantled the idea of the unconscious by pointing out the inner contradictions of the whole idea. Since the concept of the lie demands a deceiver and a deceived, how can both of these exist in the same person? He stated that people have seized on the duality of conscious-subconscious to reestablish the duality of the deceiver-deceived and thereby explain the logical difficulties of bad faith—in effect, logically allowing one to lie to oneself.

Freud divided the psyche into the id and the ego; the subject is the ego, but has no privileged relation with the id. The ego may passively receive psychic facts from the id, but has to hypothesize about their meaning—thus putting itself in the position of the other in relation to the id, and even requiring the assistance of the analyst to reveal the origin of these "facts." Psychic illness arises with the complex, which is apparently on the side of the ego, because it is an entity symbolically trying to break out into the light. The censor, however, prevents these psychic facts in question from becoming a part of the consciousness of the ego by repressing them. And it is this censor, the superego, the *Über ich*, that Sartre found illogical. For if this censor is going to repress something, it must be conscious of what it is repressing; it must let through the legitimate impulses into clear consciousness while holding back those detrimental to the well-being of the ego. How can it make this choice, then, if it is not conscious of the psychic events in the unconscious, conscious of the condemned drives of the id, conscious of their impact on the ego, and therefore conscious of its own activity? "En un mot, comment la censure discernerait-elle les impulsions refoulables sans avoir conscience de les discerner? Peut-on concevoir un savoir qui serait ignorance de soi?"[2] The logical functioning of the trinity id-ego-superego therefore collapses, and, as a result of the necessary functioning of the superego, the unified psyche has got logically to be conscious. What has psychoanalysis done? "Elle a simplement localisé cette double activité de répulsion et d'attraction au niveau de la censure."[3]

The proponents of the unconscious have therefore taken consciousness away from the ego because it could not explain what Sartre would call "mauvaise foi," and transferred it to the censor, the *Über ich*, as if that explained something more. What they have done, in effect, is the same thing the moon-philosopher accuses men of having done in Cyrano's *Voyage dans la lune*: because they were incapable of understanding the eternity of the world, they gave eternity to God, as if it were easier to imagine it in one than in the other. Why would it be easier to imagine consciousness on the part of the superego than the ego? The scope of this study does not involve discussion of the merits or demerits of Freud, but it is obvious that Sartre's philosophy could not tolerate an aspect of the psyche which lay outside consciousness, for then a man could not be free or responsible: he would stand in the same relation to an important aspect of himself as does the Other.

Does this mean, then, that the surrealist is not free if he accepts the existence of the subconscious? Georges Bataille offers an answer to this question, an answer hardly suitable to Sartre: he gives us a definition of liberty as a free activity of the mind. This free activity would be betrayed if we subordinated it to a preconceived plan. In effect the surrealist decision is not to decide any longer (a handy decision if we believe that a large part of our psyche lies outside the consciousness).

La différence profonde du surréalisme avec l'existentialisme de Jean-Paul Sartre tient à ce caractère d'*existence* de la liberté. Si je ne l'asservis pas la liberté *éxistera*:

c'est la poésie, les mots, n'ayant plus à servir à quelque désignation utile, se déchaînent et ce déchaînement est l'image de *l'existence libre*, qui n'est jamais donné que dans l'instant.[4]

Human activity for Sartre is intentional, goal-directed; surrealist activity here seems to be gratuitous. This distinction between existential and surrealist activity is, as we shall see, parallel to Sartre's distinction between prose and poetry.

Le Mur

The five stories in *Le Mur* demonstrate the various efforts of five lives to escape the human condition; each flight is stopped by a wall because "fuir l'Existence, c'est encore exister."[5] In varying degrees of explicitness, they are devoted to discrediting the various themes of surrealism, or the various ways in which the surrealists approached the problem of man's condition; we will study them in the order of their richness and obviousness and comment on those themes: (1) "L'Enfance d'un chef," a large section of which is dedicated to an obvious satire on several aspects of the surrealist movement; (2) "Erostrate," a consideration of the *acte surréaliste*; (3) "La Chambre," the use of abnormal mental states; (4) "Intimité," a treatment of love; and (5) "Le Mur," the consent to one's death, i.e., suicide.

I would not present the last three of these stories, in the order given above, as intentional comments by Sartre on surrealism. However, it is no less interesting to point out that the surrealist effort to escape man's condition valued these very "techniques," and that with them the surrealists conceived the possibility of escaping it to that utopia of unification of opposites mentioned by Breton in the *Second manifeste*. Sartre, on the other hand, believed in no such paradise, or even in its possibility, and, as we shall see, made human consciousness dependent on keeping the opposites distinct. Thus, although the first two stories are fairly obvious in their comment, the criticism of surrealism in the last three is only implied, and reflects the basic difference between the surrealist and Sartrean approaches to man's condition: one will seek ways to resolve, to neutralize it and its anguish; the other will insist on facing it and showing the bankruptcy of efforts to escape it. For if we could escape it, then we would no longer be forced to be free; if we unified our opposites, we would weaken the *pour-soi*.

The stories in *Le Mur* are certainly more than criticisms of surrealism—they are literature in their own right, and dramatizations of Sartre's beliefs. Since Sartre was not a surrealist, it turns out naturally enough that his stories were implicit remarks on the surrealist attitudes.

"*L'Enfance d'un chef*"

Critics frequently refer to this story, wherein Lucien Fleurier seeks his identity in the definitions given to him by another, as a demonstration of *mauvaise foi*. And, although bad faith and lack of authenticity are Lucien's main characteristics, the story is more than a dramatization of some Sartrean ideas: it is also a kind of intellectual history of the interwar years, a survey of the options open to a young man, and a satire on some of the major ideologies of the time including Barresian regional mysticism (there is an amusing pastiche of the Barresian style), *L'Action française*, and various aspects of surrealism which will concern us in this section.

Lucien is first exposed to surrealism and Freud by his fellow *lycéen*, Berliac; from this moment until he breaks off his relation with the surrealist Bergère, the story is an almost continuous mockery of surrealism, and reads like a burlesque history of the movement, its occupations and preoccupations.

Berliac writes poetry ("Caruso gobait des yeux crus tous les soirs . . .") by the new technique of "écriture automatique." This poetry disconcerts Lucien, who suddenly feels the great desire to kill himself. Suicide was, of course, one of the important concerns of the surrealist and dadaist group: Jacques Vaché and René Crevel could be cited as heroes and models. Aragon, in his treatment of suicide, admonished those who only threatened and carried a pistol in their pocket: "N'insultez pas au vrai suicide par ce perpétuel halètement. . . ."[6] But when Lucien asks Berliac for advice, the latter answers like a dadaist: "Fais comme tu voudras . . . ça n'a aucune importance . . . Rien n'a jamais aucune importance."[7]

Berliac invites Lucien to lunch at his mother's apartment and while he is there mouthes another favorite claim of the dadaist-surrealist group: ". . . les vraies victimes de la guerre c'est nous." (163) Lucien agrees that they are both of a "génération sacrifiée," thus indulging in a little latter-day romanticism. Later, as they smoke English cigarettes and listen to American records, Berliac initiates Lucien to psychoanalysis. Berliac admits that he has lusted after his mother since he was 15 years old and Lucien is forced to admit that he also wanted to sleep with his mother. However, Lucien is a little uncomfortable by the thought of Berliac's mother, because she has warts and a birthmark on her face. The amusing implication here is that Freud's theories make you desire your mother even if she is repulsive, not only involving you in potential incest, but destroying your esthetic discernment.

There is a certain scientific interest for Lucien in these confidences, and he is prompted to read Freud's work. It is ironic that the surrealist's approach to automatism has a certain scientific intention: the attempt to dig into the subconscious by a nonlogical technique was considered a kind of research that Breton emphasized, condemning those who used automatic writing as a facile estheticism, a tool for artistic creation. In the *Second manifeste* (1929) he took the surrealists to task for neglecting the experimental, scientific, and disciplined aspect of surrealism in favor of artistic satisfaction.

Lucien and Berliac therefore take up the most delicate subjects with objectivity, just as the surrealists did in their own analyses of sexual matters in their journals. They decide that they have complexes and get into the habit of interpreting their dreams and their least gestures. Berliac has such a rich dream life that Lucien suspects him of fabrication. Obviously such proceedings lend themselves to dishonesty and pretense. Desnos, who had a great facility in expressing himself in "sommeils hypnotiques" or other subconscious fashions, was suspected of pretending.[8] The popularity of dream interpretation and analysis with the surrealists is too well known to warrant much discussion; reports on dreams were a regular part of *La Révolution surréaliste*, or *Le Surréalisme au service de la révolution*. Sartre uses Lucien and Berliac to reduce dream interpretation to a kind of adolescent game.

Lucien is, on the whole, rather satisfied with his newfound complexes, because he no longer has to "chercher dans sa conscience les manifestations palpables de son caractère." (165) He knows that the real Lucien is in his subconscious, and is therefore relieved to give up his freedom and responsibility. He is somewhat proud that there are monsters lurking in his subconscious, that he is not just another uninteresting fellow, that there is more to him than meets the eye. "Il y a toujours autre chose," says Berliac enigmatically. (165) Lucien writes a poem which they memorize; they finally reduce it to its first words, "les crabes," which they say, winking at each other, to express secretly their mutual knowledge of their complexes. Thus surrealism is presented as a means for rejecting responsibility, for lending oneself an air of sinister but artificial profundity, and is again reduced to an adolescent game, a secret language for schoolboys.

Lucien had given up his "pratiques solitaires" for six months because he was too busy. But when he considers that Freud warned in his books of the dangers of repressing what was natural, that neurosis could be the result of breaking one's habits too suddenly, he resumes them. It may very well be true that repression of normal drives results in neurosis, but here Sartre is making Freud a justification for masturbation. If we define masturbation as the derivation of satisfaction from oneself alone, then the technique of automatism with the sufficiency of the individual to practice it very nearly approaches that definition.

Lucien wonders if they may not go mad. In fact, on Thursdays, they seem to be near madness—after having smoked entire packages of "cigarettes opiacées." One may well ask if the "madness" was not more a result of the cigarettes than the effect of their surreal experiences. Madness, again, was one of the preoccupations of the surrealists, as we will have occasion to point out.

No one was more sensitive to "la beauté pathétique du complexe d'Oedipe," as Sartre ironically put it, than Lucien. But he is different from Berliac:

> . . . il y voyait surtout le signe d'une puissance de passion qu'il souhaitait dériver plus tard vers d'autres fins. Berliac au contraire semblait se complaire dans son état et n'en voulait pas sortir. "Nous sommes des types foutus, disait-il avec orgueil, des ratés. Nous ne ferons jamais rien. (166)

Berliac then is more of a dadaist. He is content to experience his "complex" for its own sake, with no goal in mind. Lucien is a budding surrealist. At this particular point in the story, he is somewhat like Breton, who took the basic attitudes and theories of dadaism and turned them to something constructive and creative—a search for a new reality, etc. Lucien would like to take his Oedipus complex, his passion, and use it as a tool toward some goal, just as Breton would attempt to apply the procedures of dadaism. At least there is some intelligence in the surrealist position, but if we take Berliac as an example of the dadaist, we get a picture of an unsavory character: he is an adolescent who covers the pimples on his face with spittle, he peeks under the covers at his mother while she is asleep, he has no goal and takes a certain pleasure in being a *raté*; he finally disappears and is never heard from again.

Lucien is disappointed because he had counted on Berliac to get women for him: "il pensait que la possession d'une jolie maîtresse changerait tout naturellement le cours de ses idées." (167) It is quite natural that a *lycéen* should be interested in women, but one would think it would be for biological rather than for philosophical reasons. The surrealists stressed the relation between the sexes, particularly when it became *amour fou*, because it made possible a restructuring of the world of things by the power of mind, or imagination. In other words, it literally changes the course of one's ideas, as Lucien thinks. Love was a state of grace which united the possible and impossible, "la nécessité naturelle à la nécessité humaine ou logique."[9] The surrealists took this state seriously, but it lends itself to mockery: Lucien expects to take advantage of the sexual aspect of the man-woman encounter to advance himself philosophically, to get himself out of his uncertainty, to help himself with his problems of identity. The criticism of the surrealist idea of love will become quite evident when Lucien finally meets Bergère himself.

Two other points of the surrealists, the attack on the family and the bourgeoisie, are brought up when Berliac makes jokes about Lucien's parents, calling them "monsieur et madame Dumollet." Lucien understood that "un surréaliste méprisât la bourgeoisie en général," (167) but he is annoyed that Berliac does not have the simple decency to show some respect toward Madame Fleurier, who had received him with friendship.

At last the day comes when Lucien meets the surrealist Bergère himself: monsieur Achille Bergère. It is probably no accident that his name has the same rhythm and the same initials as André Breton. He is not described exactly like André Breton, but closely enough to be recognizable: he was around 35 years old (Breton was 42 in 1938 when the story was finished) and had magnificent white hair (Breton had long thick hair, although the pictures taken about that time do not show it to be white).

Bergère's demeanor is overpowering: he takes Lucien's hand and forces him to sit down. He is silent, enveloping Lucien with a "chaud regard tendre." "Etes-vous inquiet?" is his first question. Lucien blurts out his life story, or what he imagines to be the story of his Freudian complexes. He is totally overcome by the surrealist's presence. Berliac is jealous, apparently fearing that Lucien will take his place in Bergère's affections, and the latter does give all his attention to Lucien, while Berliac seethes with anger and frustration.

The description of Breton by Nadeau, and of Bergère by Sartre are very close. At this time Breton was an obvious *chef d'école*; he had such a personal magnetism that very few who had met him were not conquered. His face is massive, writes Nadeau, noble, majestic; there is a feeling that goes directly from his heart to yours. Although he is youthful, "il rit rarement et a le geste sobre." All those who meet him love him.

> Ceux qui goûtent avec lui des minutes d'amitié inoubliables, et il ne les marchande à personne, sont prêts à tout lui sacrifier: femme, maîtresses, amis, et quelques-uns les lui ont sacrifiés en effet. Ils se sont entièrement donnés à lui et au mouvement.[10]

Lucien feels as if he had just gone through an initiation ceremony. After having made his confession, Lucien asks, "Qu'est-ce qu'il faut que je fasse?'' much in the manner of the sinner asking ''What must I do to be saved?'' (Some of Breton's enemies had already referred to him as the Pope.) Bergère prescribes the reading of Rimbaud's *Illuminations* just as any surrealist might have done in the early days of the movement. In spite of the fact that the surrealists proclaimed Rimbaud one of the major ancestors of the movement, the obvious satire in having the phony Bergère give the unauthentic adolescent a copy of *Les Illuminations* is not entirely fair to Breton, who had rejected the necessity for ancestry in the *Second manifeste* in 1929: ''Rien de plus stérile, en définitive, que cette perpétuelle interrogation des morts. . . . Inutile de discuter encore sur Rimbaud: Rimbaud s'est trompé, Rimbaud a voulu nous tromper.''[11]

Bergère drops Berliac for Lucien just as Breton himself often had inexplicable preferences, astonishing changes in attitude, sudden antipathies and sympathies, and Lucien goes to visit the surrealist almost every day. Bergère's apartment is furnished, just as one might expect, with strange objects: a spiked chastity belt, plaster breasts with little spoons implanted in them, a stolen monk's skull used as a paper weight. There are negro statuettes (the cubists, immediate parents of the surrealists-dadaists, were the first to consider primitive sculpture in other than an anthropological way), a large bronze louse, and the walls are covered with announcements of the death of ''le surréaliste Bergère.'' (It was not uncommon for a surrealist's surrealist enemies to announce his death in the journals.) There are ''des poufs dont le siège de velours rouge reposait sur des jambes de femmes en bois peint,'' and it is amusing to note that such an item, called ''l'Ultra-immeuble''[12] was constructed by Kurt Seligman and exhibited at the highly successful Exposition Internationale du Surréalisme in Paris in January 1938, a few months before ''L'Enfance d'un chef'' was finished. It is not particularly important whether Sartre got the idea there or not, but he had the opportunity, since he had begun teaching at the lycée Pasteur in the fall of 1937.

Bergère also has several *farces* and *attrapes* which he keeps on a shelf: ''Poudre à éternuer, poil à gratter, sucre flottant, étron diabolique, jarretelle de la mariée,'' etc. (172) Before Lucien's charmed eyes, he picks up the ''étron diabolique'' and gravely states: ''Ces attrapes ont une valeur révolutionnaire; elles inquiètent. Il y a plus de puissance destructrice en elles que dans les oeuvres complètes de Lénine. (172) This is basically what the surrealists claimed for the *objet surréaliste* or the *méthode critique-paranoïaque*, but the ludicrous object Bergère uses, and the astonishing exaggeration that it is more powerful than the works of Lenin, cheapens and satirizes a serious surrealist idea, interconnected with the concepts of *le hasard objectif* and the *vases communicants*, and the point where things cease to be perceived as opposites. But then satire is not meant to be unbiased, and this is not the place to argue the comparative merits of Sartrean and surreal concepts of the identity of objects. This is also an intimation of Sartre's attack on surrealism in *Qu'est-ce que la littérature?*, where he accuses the surrealists of refusing to engage in a Marxist-oriented social action—as if a practical joke could at all be comparable to a serious commitment to the revolution of the proletariat.

What is the surrealist idea satirized when Bergère says that the "étron diabolique" has a revolutionary value? It is revolutionary in the sense that the identity of objects in the external world must be broken down if we are to free man from his perceptual prejudices. If things are what they are, then man is forever separate from them in a kind of fine, safe, but restricted world of common sense. There is always the self and the external world, and the point where contradictions cease to exist (the surrealist ideal) will never come about.

Sartre explained what was supposed to be the impact of these *attrapes* in *Qu'est-ce que la littérature?*: anyone who lifted false cubes of sugar, made from marble, was supposed to feel

> dans une illumination fulgurante et instantanée, la destruction de l'essence objective du sucre par elle-même; il fallait lui procurer cette déception de tout l'être, ce malaise, ce porte-à-faux que donnent par exemple les farces-attrapes . . . A la faveur de cette intuition, on espère que le monde entier se decouvrira comme une contradiction radicale.[13]

This effect, explained Sartre, is the aim of surrealist painting and sculpture. We will go into greater detail on Sartre's criticism of the *objet surréaliste* and surrealist art in general when we study the pertinent section of *Littérature*. For the present, let us remark that surrealist activity and the *objet surréaliste*, in the person of Bergère, are reduced to a kind of cheap practical joke: sneezing and itching powder, and artificial excrement. And the *objet surréaliste*, which is supposed to aid in the destruction of subjectivity and objectivity and produce that ideal point where there is no contradiction, is given an unflattering parallel: Bergère throws the *poils à gratter* into a prostitute's bed, declaring to her that he is impotent, and leaves the room. He presents his action to Lucien as a joke, but we soon see that he is a homosexual, and guess that he really did it out of his dislike for women—not a rare attitude in a male homosexual. Surrealist revolutionary action is reduced to playing practical jokes on prostitutes.

On rereading the story with the awareness that Bergère is a homosexual, we can begin to see that he was concerned with seducing Lucien all along. "Qu'est-ce qu'il faut que je fasse?" Lucien had asked. And Bergère had answered that he should do nothing, especially not sit down.

"A moins, dit-il en riant, que ce ne soit sur un pal." The reader does not immediately see the relevance of that remark, unless he means that the sharpened stake would cause him to get right up again. But Bergère is obviously giving the image a pederastic connotation: the *pal* is not simply a sharpened stake, but also the oriental method of execution wherein the body was penetrated by a sharpened stake. Immediately after this remark, Bergère asks "Avez-vous lu Rimbaud?" Then when Lucien comes to visit him he initiates him to "le dérèglement de tous les sens," and tells him he will be saved when he can see distinctly and at will a negress on her knees sucking the obelisk at the place de la Concorde—the obvious image of fellation. Then Bergère lends him *les Chants de Maldoror* and the works of the marquis de Sade, two other major surrealist ancestors for rebellion and the omnipotence of desire—desire being for Breton the link which connects waking and dreaming, the *vases communicants*.

Lucien is shocked that Rimbaud is a homosexual, but Bergère smooths his feelings, telling him that it was simply the prime and proper *dérèglement* of his sensibility and that we owe his poems to his pederasty. This is really a bitterly satirical remark, equal to making Freud the justification for masturbation. Bergère produces photographs of old, hideously ugly, naked prostitutes, to support his point that there are not specific objects of sexual desire, that women have no priority simply because "elles ont un trou entre les jambes. . . ." (173) In reality, Bergère is simply exhibiting a not uncommon desire on the part of male homosexuals to degrade women—such pictures can be had in specialty stores in the United States today. One need not go to Bou-Saada to get them as Bergère says he did. And the attempt to reduce these women to their flesh is Sartre's definition of sadism.

Immediately following this scene, we find a lacerating satire of the surrealist idea of desire. Surrealism proclaimed the omnipotence of desire, and the legitimacy of its realization; the marquis de Sade became the central figure in its pantheon. It was he who carried the application of desire to its extreme limits: his unwavering adherence to gratification made him a kind of hero of desire for the surrealists. Freud had made the libido "le moteur essentiel des pensées et actes humains,"[14] and considered society's restrictions far from being always profitable. Bergère does not really have to have much imagination if he has read *Les 120 Journées de Sodome* when he proclaims that every object can be an object of sexual desire: "Moi, j'ai fait l'amour avec des mouches. J'ai connu un fusilier marin qui couchait avec des canards." (173) But the point here is that the ubiquity and legitimacy of the surrealist desire are used as the justification for having sexual relations with animals. The fact that the ducks died and were eaten by the bataillon is an idea taken with a little change from Sade.

Lucien is somewhat upset by all this.

"Etre seul! gémissait-il en se tordant les mains, n'avoir personne pour me conseiller, pour me dire si je suis dans le droit chemin." S'il allait jusqu'au bout, s'il pratiquait pour de bon, le dérèglement de tous ses sens, est-ce qu'il n'allait pas perdre pied et se noyer? Un jour que Bergère lui avait longtemps parlé d'André Breton, Lucien murmura comme dans un rêve, "Oui, mais si, après ça, je ne peux plus revenir en arrière?" (173)

This is an interesting quotation stylistically because the phrase "Un jour que Bergère lui avait longtemps parlé d'André Breton" does not fit. It is stuck into the musings and fears of Lucien, and seems almost irrelevant. The result is that the phrase jolts the reader, just as it was meant to do: Sartre wanted to mention Breton at this point in the story, just as he had "longtemps parlé d'Achille Bergère." It is the only time Breton is mentioned in this long story, and comes just as Bergère has been introduced and exposed his "surrealist" theories. If we are not meant to take it as an outright identification of Achille Bergère, at least it was meant as a very strong association.

It is not my intention to suggest that Breton was homosexual, but at the time, the accusation was made. Paul Claudel's letter in 1925 stated: "Quant aux mouvements actuels, pas un seul ne peut conduire à une véritable rénovation ou création. Ni le dadaisme, ni le surréalisme qui ont un seul sens: pédérastique."[15] Whether he meant the term literally, or figuratively to indicate a sterile, unsavory little society of mutual admirers, the word is still there. Breton was not allowed to make a speech at the Congress of Writers for the Defense of Culture in 1935 because he had struck Ilya Ehrenbourg in the street: the Russian delegate had called surrealist activity *pédérastique*. Jacques Prévert said of Breton: "Et tous ces hommes l'ont aimé follement: comme une femme."[16] Breton would never pardon Maurice Martin du Gard for describing him in *les Nouvelles littéraires* (1924) as ". . . un mage. Peut-être bien un peu un mage d'Epinal, avec sur ses fidèles l'autorité magnétique d'un Oscar Wilde."[17] Nadeau, reporting on the surrealist discussions in 1928 of sexual pleasure, writes that love among men was almost unanimously condemned, "Breton en tête, et nous y insistons afin de casser les reins à une *légende tenace*."[18] [My emphasis]

Lucien becomes Rimbaud, come to Paris to see Verlaine-Bergère. M. and Mme. Fleurier, fine bourgeois people (Lucien's father owns a small factory), invite Bergère to dinner, and find him totally charming; even the maid likes him: she had never seen such a "bel homme." It may seem ironic that the surrealist is so acceptable to the bourgeois, but we can see a comment on this situation in the postwar *Littérature*. That systematic destruction by surrealism never goes any further than scandal, wrote Sartre. "La bourgeoisie laisse faire; elle sourit de ces étourderies. Peu lui importe que l'écrivain la méprise. . . ." This scorn will never go very far because the bourgeoisie is the surrealist's only public. Besides, continued Sartre, the bourgeoisie knows that the writer is on its side, and that he needs it "pour justifier son esthétique d'opposition et de ressentiment. . . ."[19] It is even his accomplice in a sense: "Il vaut mieux contenir les forces de négation dans un vain esthétisme. . . ."[20] It would probably prefer the literature of Bordeaux or Bourget, but it finds nothing wrong with useless books that turn the mind away from serious preoccupations. Thus the status quo is not disturbed and literature becomes only an abstract negation, even when it is most insulting. And surrealism is defanged: "Ce n'est que de la littérature."

Bergère is indulging in what Sartre called "le merveilleux surréaliste." He makes a defiant gesture, puts the world between parentheses, and then goes ahead and loves life. He is a Grand Meaulnes radicalized.[21] He must save himself, but without undue provocation, "sans renoncer aux avantages de sa position."[22] This is what Bergère does: he is a charmer of the bourgeoisie, a nephew of General Nizan (whom M. Fleurier knows), evidently a "fils de famille," as Sartre called the surrealist; he scorns and seeks to astonish the bourgeoisie, but is quite acceptable to it.

The surrealist episode of "L'Enfance d'un chef" ends with the homosexual seduction of Lucien during a trip to Normandy, during which he plans to excuse his dirty feet by remarking on bourgeois ideas of cleanliness, making surrealism an excuse for being unkempt.

"L'Enfance" is a very dense story in its references and implications: there are no sentences that do not add to the meaning and total impact. The offhand reader may simply accept Bergère as a fairly typical surrealist because he mouthes (however superficially) what seem to be authentic theories of the movement, he knows the proper ancestors, he has the proper attitudes. The fact that he was a homosexual does not appear to indict the whole movement. But on closer reading, we begin to see that all the trappings and theories of the surrealists that Bergère explained (and the theories were authentic *as far as they went*) were simply an apology for and an approach to homosexuality and the seduction of Lucien. It is not difficult to miss this aspect of the story if one is concentrating on "Enfance" as a dramatization of existential authenticity and bad faith.

The narrative technique in this story,[23] leaving Lucien a maximum of freedom from an omniscient author, lets us identify more easily with him; and the seriousness and difficulty of Sartrean ideas tend to moss over the satirical aspects. But what we had not at first noticed, on second reading becomes by that fact even sharper, and on the third or fourth reading we feel the satire to be even bitter.

"Erostrate"

Surrealism was one of the evident subjects of "L'Enfance," but it is not specifically mentioned in "Erostrate." Our problem here is to determine then to what extent Paul Hilbert, the protagonist and narrator of "Erostrate," is a surrealist. Hilbert is a functionary who buys a pistol and plans to kill six people indiscriminately in the street, retire to his apartment, await the police, and commit suicide just as they arrive to apprehend him. He writes identical letters attacking humanism and mails them to 102 French writers. He goes out to fire into the crowd, but he is so nervous and distraught that he succeeds in shooting only one man, and that practically through fear and by accident. He misses the street that leads home and takes refuge in the restroom of a restaurant. Although he puts the pistol barrel into his mouth, he is unable to fire, throws out his gun, and surrenders.

His plan is precisely to perform the *acte surréaliste* as it is defined by Breton in the *Second manifeste*:

> L'acte surréaliste le plus simple consiste, revolver aux poings, à descendre dans la rue et à tirer au hasard, tant qu'on peut, dans la foule. Qui n'a pas eu, au moins une fois, envie d'en finir de la sorte avec le petit système d'avilissement et de crétinisation en vigueur a sa place toute marquée dans cette foule, ventre à hauteur de canon.[24]

Such an act sounds very brutal, to say the least. In *Littérature*, Sartre will use it to accuse the surrealists of sporadic, disorganized acts of violence in the service of the revolution, of reducing violence to an absolute, of accepting it as an end, and of social irresponsibility. In the re-edition of the *Manifestes du surréalisme* in 1946 Breton defended himself rather unconvincingly:

> Cet acte que je dis le plus simple, il est clair que mon intention n'est pas de le recommander entre tous parce qu'il est simple et me chercher querelle à ce propos revient à demander bourgeoisement à tout non-conformiste pourquoi il ne se suicide pas, à tout révolutionnaire pourquoi il ne va pas vivre en U.R.S.S.[25]

Breton apparently got this idea of the *acte surréaliste* from the behavior of Jacques Vaché 10 years earlier, and reported in *Les Pas perdus*. When Breton had gone to the premiere of Apollinaire's *Les Mamelles de Tirésias*, he had seen Vaché causing a great disturbance in the orchestra: "Il était entré dans la salle revolver au poing et il parlait de tirer à balles sur le public."[26]

Paul Hilbert has, in fact, some resemblances to Vaché: he intends to fire into a theatre crowd as they leave the presentation. He did not like to shake hands; he was friendly with his co-workers, "bien que j'eusse horreur de leur serrer la main . . . ils avaient une façon obscène de déculotter leur main. . . ." Breton writes that Vaché "ne tendait la main pour dire ni bonjour ni au revoir."[27] Hilbert remarks, "Je n'ai jamais eu de commerce intime avec une femme." And Breton reports that although Vaché had a mistress, "A l'en croire, il n'avait avec elle aucun rapport sexuel et se contentait de dormir près d'elle, dans le même lit."[28] It is not of great importance to identify a real-life model for Hilbert, but it is difficult to attribute these resemblances to pure accident.

But there is a more interesting question of Hilbert's identity: What is he? Is he surrealist or existentialist? Or is he neither? Contat and Rybalka write: "La lettre que Paul Hilbert adresse aux écrivains dans "Erostrate" n'est-elle pas la condamnation la plus radicale que nous ayons de l'humanisme chez Sartre?"[29] Immediately above they had quoted Sartre's *prière d'insérer* to the effect that one cannot reject the human condition by a crime, yet they seem to be making the criminal Hilbert a spokesman for Sartre. Certainly Hilbert's letter to the 102 French writers sounds like a Sartrean indictment of a facile, superficial humanism, the kind the self-taught man practices in *La Nausée*. But this Hilbert is no lucid Roquentin, no searching intellectual like Mathieu. Still, is there any reason why Sartre could not choose a neurotic criminal to state an opinion?

The answer to this question is that Hilbert is surrealist material. He is the kind of disaffected person who might have come into the offices of the journal *La Révolution surréaliste*, of the species Gengenbach,[30] and had his letter published. Sartre, in effect, demonstrated the wrong reaction to the human condition, i.e., the surrealist reaction. Hilbert's revolt against the facile humanism is portrayed as naive, childish, and destructive; in a word, surrealist. It is the same "humanism" against which Roquentin speaks, and for this reason the unwary reader immediately assumes Hilbert is speaking for Sartre. The confusion comes from the fact that surrealism and existentialism face a few common problems, one of which is the dislike of traditional ideas of humanism. But Sartre showed here that the surrealist revolt is violent, petulant, ridiculous, cowardly, and completely ineffective; by implication, the existentialist revolt is sober, intellectual, tragic, and if not totally effective, at least courageous.

It is easy to see Roquentin as the first lucid step toward authenticity; as that step into despair, the other side of which life may begin; as the beginning of the effort to live with absurdity in dignity. But Hilbert is like a character from Céline—it seems that he has perceived absurdity, but he will never do much more than wallow about in it, vaguely ridiculous.

Thus, rather than see Hilbert as a mouthpiece for Sartre, we should understand that existentialism and surrealism share a common point, that a man who can do the "acte surréaliste le plus simple" can have the same idea an existentialist does, and that Sartre is showing how not to approach a valid problem.

So Hilbert quits his job (surrealists, according to Breton, were not supposed to be engaged in any productive activity), and eats up his savings. As we read his story, we can see that he is paranoid, that he is hardly average sexually, and we are a little surprised by the lucidity and fluency of his letter to the authors; it is full of statements of the function of language and literature, and a critique of humanity in general. This letter deserves to be taken up in detail, since it is the basis for the assertion that Sartre attacks humanism through Hilbert.

Hilbert analyzes the writers' success: they loved man, even the marvelous five-fingered hand with the opposable thumb, and so it was easy for them to find the proper way to speak to man of himself. The public threw themselves on these books and were consoled for being ugly, cowardly, cuckolded, and for not having got a raise the first of the year. It is easy to see that Hilbert has got a higher idea of the function of literature, just as years later, Sartre will assert in *Littérature* that writing is a valid commitment, that it is action. This does not make Hilbert any more a spokesman for Sartre, for Breton also in the first part of the *Premier manifeste* asserts that realism is "hostile à tout essor intellectuel et moral." He therefore attacks the novel as the privileged form of literature, a form which reduced literature to a kind of recreation, to a game of *piquet*.

Hilbert continues with his explanation of why he cannot love men. "Mais je vous dis que je ne *peux pas* les aimer." (81) He would rather watch seals eat than watch a man at dinner. The 102 French writers may find in that man's expression the vigilance of the Spirit, but "moi ça m'écoeure: je ne sais pas pourquoi; je suis né ainsi." This reasoning is the same as that Sartre gave to the anti-Semite who is willing to admit that his attitude is nonlogical: ". . . l'antisémitisme se présente comme une passion."[31] It is the same as that of Lucien Fleurier from "Enfance": "Mais qu'est-ce que tu veux, c'est plus fort que moi, je ne peux pas les toucher, c'est physique. . . ." (216) This nonreason for condemning humanism is not one Sartre would accept—another reason, it seems to me, for not accepting Hilbert as Sartre's spokesman.

Hilbert's anti-humanism, then, is not a refusal to pattern himself after a definition concocted by a crowd of *salauds*, by the unauthentic; not a refusal to subject his existence to an essence or to subscribe to the *esprit du sérieux*. He says he does not like men and that therefore "je suis un misérable et je ne puis trouver de place au soleil." (81) We have to accept his rather romantic explanation ("je suis né ainsi"), or assume that his anti-humanism is merely the result of personal failure.

As we have seen, some of the ideas implied in this story will be developed at a later date in *Littérature* or *Réflexions sur la question juive*, and reflect Sartre's preoccupations. However distant chronologically or formally, writes Jeanson, there is "une même présence, une étroite parenté d'accent, de démarche, de ton"[32] in Sartre's works.

Hilbert's paranoia extends even to words, and we see that he will refuse to use words as tools; such a refusal qualifies him as a poet by Sartre's definition. The surrealists would also use language as a tool, but not in the Sartrean sense of a tool of communication. For the surrealist, language was supposed to be the vehicle for the surreal imagination (*Premier manifeste*), whereby the unconscious found expression. The "utilitarian" aspects of language were applied toward different goals. Hilbert feels that nothing belongs to him:

> les mots par exemple: j'aurais voulu des mots *à moi*. Mais ceux dont je dispose ont trainé dans je ne sais combien de consciences; ils s'arrangent tout seuls dans ma tête en vertu d'habitudes qu'ils ont prises chez les autres et ce n'est pas sans répugnance que je les utilise en vous écrivant. (82)

This remark fits curiously with a quotation Sartre drew from Francis Ponge in an essay in 1944:

> N'en déplaises aux paroles elles-mêmes, étant donné les habitudes que dans tant de bouches infectes elles ont contractées, il faut un certain courage pour se décider non seulement à écrire mais même à parler.[33]

This attitude toward language puts Hilbert nearer the surrealist than a committed existentialist, but again his desire to have words of his own is presented as the selfish desire of an alienated man—not as in the case of Ponge, as the effort to break through some "semantic thickness."

The letter ends with the recommendation to read tomorrow's papers, and a poet's insult to prose: "Vous savez mieux que personne ce que vaut la prose des grands quotidiens." Hilbert relishes the report that will appear in the papers, because he hopes to astonish the world, a surrealist concern. After having forced the prostitute to perform at gunpoint, he had congratulated himself on astonishing her, "et ça ne s'étonne pas facilement, une putain." (77) And as he goes downstairs after this encounter, "Voilà ce que je voudrais, les étonner tous." Like the surrealist Bergère of "Enfance," he exercises his "surrealist" tendencies on prostitutes.

Crime is not an effective rejection of the human condition, according to Sartre. And the "acte surréaliste le plus simple" is a crime. Breton wrote in the *Second manifeste* that surrealism was not afraid to make for itself "un dogme de la révolte absolue, de l'insoumission totale, du sabotage en règle, et qu'il n'attende encore rien que de la violence."[34] Hilbert dreamed of being the great criminal: "Moi, j'aime les héros noirs," he tells his office companions, a statement characteristic of the surrealist admiration for Rimbaud and Lautréamont. In Lautréamont the surrealists saw a "Moi qui s'exalte dans le sentiment de la négation absolue à l'égard de la réalité naturelle et humaine,"[35] and this negation of a society or a culture considered to be no longer valid is one of the intentions of the *acte surréaliste*.

Hilbert expected some personal satisfaction from his act: he anticipated it would change his "laideur trop humaine," that it would cut his life in two, that it would be, in effect, an irreversible act which would raise him out of his commonness to that point where the great criminal merges with the great hero. He studies the photographs of two sisters, before and after the crime they had committed, and in the wrinkles of their faces, changed by their crime and incarceration, he seems to perceive a horrible nobility that he hopes will be imprinted on his own face by his crime. The interesting point for this particular study is that Hilbert has apparently been reading surrealist journals. *Le Surréalisme au service de la révolution* in 1933 published these very pictures with the following comment:

Les soeurs Papin furent élevées au couvent du Mans. Puis leur mère les plaça dans une maison "bourgeoise" de cette ville. Six ans, elles endurèrent avec la plus parfaite soumission observations, exigences, injures. La crainte, la fatigue, l'humiliation, enfantaient lentement en elles la haine, cet alcool très doux qui console en secret car il promet à la violence de lui adjoindre, tôt ou tard, la force physique.

Le jour venu, Léa et Christine Papin rendirent sa monnaie au mal, une monnaie de fer rouge. Elles massacrèrent littéralement leurs patronnes, leur arrachant les yeux, leur écrasant la tête. Puis elles se lavèrent soigneusement et, delivrées, indifférentes, se couchèrent. La foudre était tombée, le bois brûlé, le soleil définitivement éteint.

Sortie tout armées d'un chant de Maldoror . . .
 					Paul Eluard
 					et Benjamin Péret[36]

The photographs themselves bear the caption "Sorties tout armées d'un chant de Maldoror." Hilbert's immediate inspiration came from the SASDLR, and from Lautréamont. (The same crime will become the basis for Genêt's *Les Bonnes*.) His description of the hair style of the Papin sisters fits exactly: "Un fer discret avait ondulé pareillement leurs cheveux," and for the "Après" photograph: "Elles avaient le cou nu des futures decapitées. . . ." But his act was as futile and embarrassing as the *affaire* Sadoul-Caupenne.[37] And as the title "Erostrate" indicates, the act had no other meaning than a selfish concern that one's name be remembered, as if that were the essence of the *acte surréaliste*, futile, meaningless, and criminal. And the gesture ends in a toilet.

"La Chambre"

Sartre described these stories as futile efforts to escape the human condition; of "La Chambre" in particular, he wrote: "Eve essaie de rejoindre Pierre dans le monde irréel et clos de la folie. En vain; ce monde n'est qu'un faux-semblant et les fous sont des menteurs."[38] This is a direct contradiction of the surrealist attitude as stated in *Nadja* and demonstrated in *l'Immaculée conception*.

In their attempt to break through the restrictive crust of rationality to that wealth of the imagination, the surrealists willingly turned to abnormal states of mind—imitated, provoked, or real. Breton remarks that madmen showed a profound detachment for our criticism, that they got great comfort from their imagination, that they rather enjoyed their delirium: "les hallucinations, les illusions, etc., ne sont pas une source de jouissance négligeable."[39] Sartre shows us a madman in "La Chambre" who does not find any enjoyment in his hallucinations; here is a madman who will die of organic causes in three years or less. He is not one of the surrealist maniacs "qui ne doivent leur internement qu'à un petit nombre d'actes légalement répréhensibles, et que, faute de ces actes, leur liberté . . . ne saurait être en jeu."[40] Sartre demonstrated that madness is more than just an eccentricity, a freedom of the imagination condemned by a shallow and insensitive bourgeoisie—it can be a disease that incapacitates and kills.

"Les confidences des fous, je passerais ma vie à les provoquer," writes Breton in the *Premier manifeste*.[41] This is just what he was doing in *Nadja*, and his intention and systematic provocation of those confidences is obvious to anyone who reads that book. When that young woman would stray from her "surreal" conversation or sketches to recount the petty details and problems of her life, Breton would become impatient and want to get back to his own preoccupations. After she had been taken to an institution he made no more attempt to communicate with her (at least he does not mention it even in the reedition of *Nadja* in 1964), and left himself open to accusations by his detractors that he had contributed to her crisis. Whatever these confidences were, they read like surrealist poems, and Pierre's ramblings in "La Chambre" sound suspiciously the same way. Speaking of the insane, Breton continued, "Ce sont gens d'une honnêteté scrupuleuse, et dont l'innocence n'a d'égale que la mienne."[42] This "honnêteté scrupuleuse" is just the opposite of "les fous sont des menteurs," and "La Chambre" reads like an anti-*Nadja*.

The climax of "La Chambre" is near the end of the story when the statues are flying about the room. Eve, try as hard as she might, cannot see them, and she lies to Pierre that she hears them. She has failed to enter that other world because she is sane, she has too much of her robust, logical father in her. She has failed because there *is* a difference between the sane and insane world, and this demonstration invalidates the major technique and intent of *L'Immaculée conception*: Breton and Eluard had wanted to prove that there is no division between "l'homme normal et l'homme dit 'anormal,' mais une simple transition, qu'il n'existe pas d'états à partir desquels on peut assurer que tel homme est fou";[43] all these differences would simply be a question of opinion, without scientific basis. The sections on "Les Possessions" of *L'Immaculée conception* (simulation of "débilité mentale, manie aiguë, paralysie générale, délire d'interprétation, démence précoce") would then be no more successful than Eve's attempt to enter Pierre's world, or no more than Breton's attempt to enter Nadja's. Nadeau's belief[44] that *L'Immaculée conception*, produced by the poetry of two men more or less well adjusted, should have upset the history of mental illness since they were able to go into an abnormal state and return to a state of equilibrium, seems rather exaggerated: feigning madness is as old as mankind.

Certainly "La Chambre" is not a close-knit satire on the surrealist use of abnormal mental states, but there are some curious remarks in the story which go beyond the general point that madness is no refuge from the human condition. Eve must have loved Pierre, and perhaps she still does. At times now though, she feels oppressed by him and has to force herself to enter the room. She has other reasons, it seems, for staying with him. She is revolting against her father and all he stands for: good health, optimism, success, respectability, security, normality—all good bourgeois virtues. As her father ends his weekly visit, she closes the door behind him with "Je voudrais qu'il meure." And as she realizes that she will never be able to perceive objects the way Pierre does, she comforts herself with the belief that she has at least gone beyond her father's pedestrian understanding: "Pourtant, se dit-elle avec angoisse, je ne les vois plus tout à fait comme lui." (59) It is impossible at this point not to remember Sartre's remark on the surrealist revolt: these young bourgeois wanted to ruin culture because they had been acculturated, their principal

enemy was Heine's philistine, Monnier's Prudhomme, Flaubert's bourgeois, "bref leur papa."[45]

Eve's father is a man of great common sense and robust health, just
the opposite of his wife, who lies in bed of an unknown illness, eating
pastry and remarking on how "la maladie affine les sensations"—an idea
right out of Huysmans and the Decadence and apparently adopted by the
surrealists.[46] He finds it ridiculous to "consulter un malade" about anything, and thinks Pierre would be better off with his own kind; they are
like children anyway, and better off together, "ils forment une espèce de
franc-maçonnerie." (40) Breton believed that disturbed people were more
likely to get better if they were around healthy people, and that closing
them up with other madmen only confirmed their madness and made it
irremediable.[47] "J'ai horreur des êtres malsains," says her father, but the
surrealists followed them around and imitated them; Nadja was so frail
she hardly touched the ground as she walked.[48] Several times M. Darbedat
expresses his distrust of the insane, concluding with "On ne doit jamais
entrer dans le délire d'un malade." (48)

Pierre, the madman, like the surrealist, has a special relationship
with objects. We will discuss this point at greater length in later sections
of this study, but suffice it to say for the present that Pierre's perception
of objects is very much like the Daliesque *critique-paranoïa*, where objects lose their stability and frequently become threatening. As we have
seen, Eve had not achieved this level of perception, and it was to Pierre
alone that "les choses montraient leur vrai visage." (59) The fork grows
claws and must be picked up by the middle to avoid pinches, and later
on Pierre admits that there was hardly anything wrong with the fork,
"J'ai fait ça pour effrayer le type," a surrealist preoccupation. Pierre
invents the "ziuthre," which sounds suspiciously like an *objet surréaliste*.
He has stuck pieces of cardboard together, in such a way that they re-
semble a spider, and has written some cryptic words on them. That is
used as a warning device against the attacks of flying statues, and serves
in effect the same function as the *objet surréaliste*: to break through the
ordinary world and permit some communication with the world beyond,
to weaken the barrier between reason and nonreason.

Pierre's speech sounds at times like automatic writing, and at the
end of the story the word "récapitulation" comes out totally automati-
cally by his own admission: "ce n'est pas de ce mot-là . . . Il est venu
. . . il est venu . . . J'avais l'autre sur le bout de la langue . . . et celui-là
. . . s'est mis à sa place." Suddenly he had looked foolish and the word
had appeared: automatism then is meaningless—a tongue not connected
to a conscious mind says nothing lucid. Speech becomes automatic when
the brain deteriorates.

"L'Intimité" and "Le Mur"

These two stories reflect Sartre's attitudes toward two of the surrealist's major themes: love and suicide. For a surrealist, the title "Intimité" is ironic. The story shows us some less exalted reasons for intimacy between a man and a woman, a relationship which is a far cry from *amour fou*, which was supposed to be a revolutionary force, a state of grace which united the possible and impossible, waking and dreaming.

The surrealist ideal is the romantic ideal pushed to its logical extreme. This kind of love is for the aristocrats of sensitivity and understanding, not to mention physical health. The accusation by Sartre that surrealism is just another "déclassement d'en haut,"[49] a utopic and abstract approach to man's problems, is well demonstrated in this story. Lulu and Henri are fairly ordinary people. The depth of character, physical completeness, and existential awareness for such a thing as "total" love are lacking. Whereas the surrealist *amour fou* is an ideal, "Intimité" is a look at real people with all their faults and weaknesses—weaknesses which in many cases make such an ideal simply impossible. Henri is totally impotent sexually; Lulu is satisfied with his condition because she has vague lesbian tendencies, is ashamed of her body, hates the feeling that men dominate her, and takes sexual pleasure mainly in masturbation. "Ce que c'est sale l'amour," she says. (97) Their intimacy is based on a kind of mutual emotional dependency.

Although Lulu is promised the good life on the Mediterranean by her lover, a successful and virile man who apparently has some affection for her, she cannot accept it. Her attempt to accept the plans of Rirette and Pierre for her were in bad faith. "Lulu se ment: entre soi et le regard qu'elle ne peut pas ne pas jeter sur soi, elle essaie de glisser une brume légère. En vain, la brume devient sur-le-champ transparence; on ne se ment pas: on croit qu'on se ment."[50] So she returns to Henri. She recognizes that she does not really want to go off to Nice with Pierre, that what would appear to be an idyllic situation does not correspond to her needs, and goes back to that rather pitiful but satisfying life with Henri. People live together as they can, sometimes forming bonds of intimacy on less than *amour fou*. One does not escape from existence for it would be a rare love that promised a state of grace.

Pablo Ibbieta in the first story, "Le Mur," is also trapped in a situation from which there is no issue. Captured by the fascists and forced to reveal the location of his friend or face death, he lies and accepts death. After he has accepted it in his own mind, he loses his feelings of affection for his mistress and even for the friend for whom he is dying. The memories he once called good or bad can no longer be so qualified. He has cut himself off from life. He no longer fears the threats of his captors: "Il en faut beaucoup plus pour intimider un homme qui va mourir." (31) Pablo, in effect, believes he has escaped the human condition by rejecting life, committing a kind of moral suicide.

As we have already remarked, suicide was a major preoccupation of the early surrealists and dadaists. Number two of *La Révolution surréaliste* in 1925 discussed this question: "Le suicide est-il une solution." Answers were printed for and against, the most telling being that of René Crevel, who, indeed, asphyxiated himself 10 years later. People kill themselves, he said, who cannot struggle against a certain sensation in the mind, so intense it must be taken for the truth. "Seule cette sensation permet d'accepter la plus vraisemblablement juste et définitive des solutions: le suicide."[51] At the time of Vaché's suicide it was felt that he had heroically demonstrated his scorn for an untenable state of affairs. Vaché apparently became superior to the human condition as did Pablo.

But Ibbieta's acceptance of death did him little good: existence still intruded on him. His friend was found by coincidence in the cemetery, and Pablo's life was spared. No man can understand his own death or use it to solve the problems of his life. Pablo, wrote Sartre, "voudrait jeter sa pensée de l'autre côté de l'Existence et concevoir sa propre mort. En vain."[52] That kind of attitude toward death, closely related to stoicism, does not solve the problem. The destruction of that existence or the acceptance of the termination of that existence offers no solution. "L'Existence est un plein que l'homme ne peut quitter."[53]

In these five stories we have seen explicit or implicit comments on many aspects of surrealism: the subconscious mind, automatism, *l'objet surréaliste*, *l'acte surréaliste*, abnormal mental states, love, suicide, and of the *chef d'école* himself. These walls by which the characters of *Le Mur* are blocked are not considered walls by the surrealists, for whom madness, love, suicide, and violence seemed to offer a way to break through the shell of "reality."

It is perhaps irrelevant to criticize the fairness of an intentional satire, considering the intention with which the author sets out, but in the following section we shall analyze Sartre's treatment of that movement in the long essay of 1947.

Qu'est-ce que la littérature?

As we have seen in the preceding sections, Sartre did not show a great deal of admiration for surrealism. He did not approve of the attempt to escape from the human condition, and his disapproval also showed up in the section "Situation de l'écrivain en 1947" of *Littérature*, where he was at times scarcely fair to a movement which has had a marked influence on modern art and literature.

After demonstrating that the French writer is the most bourgeois of all the nationalities, he said that French authors differ from one another only in the manner in which each assumes his situation as a bourgeois: obviously we must prepare for a Marxist approach to literary history. Then he gave a tableau of contemporary literature, based on that class awareness and distinction, in which he saw three generations: pre-World War I, between the two wars, and post-World War II. Surrealism occupies the major place in the interwar generation, and existentialism is the third generation. In 1947 then, Sartre looked back on the period of surrealism as the major current in the interwar years, from the point of view of the leader of a new generation which had yet to reach its full development and to prove itself equal to the new challenges. It is to be expected that he would find a pre-World War II mentality unsuccessful and unsuitable for postwar problems, just as the surrealists found pre-World War I attitudes unsuitable for the problems of 1918. In this section we will analyze Sartre's discussion of these attitudes.

Because the search for the useful, the utilitarian, demands the conscious voluntary life, he wrote, the surrealists considered the consciousness bourgeois.[54] They had therefore to destroy the distinctions between conscious and unconscious, which meant that they were dissolving subjectivity. Sartre then defined subjectivity as the intuition of the certainty that our thoughts belong to us and only the probability that the external world is ordered on them. That is to say, subjectivity is knowing we are not the external world, and its definition comes very close to that of consciousness, for to be conscious in Sartrean terms is to be conscious of being conscious, since by Husserl's principle of intentionality consciousness must have content.[55] He then observed that thereby the surrealist rejects the entire foundation of the stoic ethic (which allowed the stoic to separate his life from the world, to maintain his dignity in himself). Every means was good for the surrealist to escape consciousness of self, therefore his situation in the world.

There is a logical difficulty here, for how can the surrealist escape his situation in the world by denying the duality on which the stoic based his escape from the situation in the world? This means that the stoic affirms subjectivity (by Sartre's definition) and separates himself from the external world to escape his situation in it, and that the surrealist denies subjectivity and achieves the same goal, or claims to.

The stoic is effectively taken out of the world. The stoics admired Socrates because of his indifference to heat and cold, food, dress, and his total indifference to bodily comforts. They believed all things to be part of one system, called Nature, and one was virtuous if one willed to be in agreement with Nature. But this virtue took no account of health, wealth, or happiness—virtue was in the will, consequently all good and evil in a man's life depended on himself. The stoic made a strict division between internal and external and thus became free of the external. The logical result of Sartre's assertion is that the stoic and the surrealist would then attempt to escape the human condition—one by separating subjectivity from the external world, the other by uniting them. How can this be?

The problem is that the stoic and the surrealist systems are not basically comparable—the conscious and unconscious or subjective and objective of the surrealist would appear to be somewhat parallel to the stoic internal and external, but the surrealist goal was unification of the two concepts in a utopic outlook, whereas the stoic goal was attaining virtue and taking advantage of the cruelties of the external world to exercise that virtue. Sartre's remark that the surrealist rejection of subjectivity knocks the props from under the stoic ethic is unclear in its intent, except as it attempts to discredit the surrealist attitude. On the other hand, Sartre did not accept the stoic ethic. True enough, the stoic ethic was based on a separation of subjectivity (particularly as will) from the external world, but the stoic was not concerned about conscious and unconscious, and Sartre's definition of subjectivity in this section has fallen very near to the idea of consciousness.

Sartre continued to the effect that surrealism subscribed to psychoanalysis because it allowed the subconscious to invade the conscious, and to automatic writing because it destroyed subjectivity and produced objects the subjectivity could not recognize as its own. (221) This is, of course, accurate, but it is not the whole story. Sartre had to attack any anti-subjectivity because he in general associated subjectivity with the *pour-soi*; any weakening of the *pour-soi* weakens consciousness and therefore lucidity. Furthermore, the beginning of Sartre's philosophy was the cogito, that is, the primitive claim of subjectivity to existence.

Thus, said Sartre, it was not a question for the surrealists of substituting their unconscious subjectivity (which, to Sartre, would be a contradiction anyway, unless we associate the term with the pre-reflective cogito, which I would hesitate to apply to the surrealists, and seems to me to be a contradiction also) for consciousness, but to show that subjectivity is an inconsistent illusion in an objective universe. But Sartre extrapolated here when he presented an "univers objectif" as the original surrealist vision of things. This "univers objectif" to which Sartre referred is the primordial universe of things in themselves, as they "actually" are before the arising of subjectivity (in Sartrean terms, the whole universe of the *en-soi* before the rise of the *pour-soi*) which he seemed to be making the surrealists use as a kind of norm or basis of reality. This is putting words into the mouths of the surrealists, for they had no conception of an objective universe where things exist in their eternal reality. And Sartre's next remark made his previous sentence irrelevant: "Mais la deuxième démarche du surréaliste est pour détruire à son tour l'objectivité." (221) He presented the surrealist as first destroying subjectivity in favor of an "univers objectif" and then destroying objectivity as if the concepts could exist separately.

One might be able to infer that such was the surrealist's intention if one considers only the *Premier manifeste* and his general behavior, but the *Second manifeste* makes it plain that subjectivity and objectivity would disappear at the same time, their definitions being dependent on each other. And this could be only an inference because the surrealists never said anything about that specific aspect of the problem. It must be bluntly admitted that the surrealist was not the trained philosopher that Sartre was, and left some things unconsidered.

How then is the surrealist to destroy subjectivity, according to Sartre? "Il s'agit de faire éclater le monde," and as no dynamite can do that and since a real destruction of the totality of existents is impossible, they will attempt to disintegrate particular objects, "c'est-à-dire d'annuler sur ces objets-témoins la structure même de l'objectivité." (221) Since they cannot do this on real existents, they will produce imaginary objects, constructed in such a way that their objectivity suppresses itself. We have already touched on this problem in the discussion of Bergère and the *étrons diaboliques* in "Enfance," and must give it greater consideration here and later on when Sartre used the *objet surréaliste* in his Marxist objections to surrealist activity in relation to the proletariat.

Sartre gave Duchamp's sugar cubes made from marble as an example; whoever picked them up was supposed to "ressentir, dans une illumination fulgurante et instantanée, la destruction de l'essence objective de sucre par elle-même." (222) We have already seen this satirized in the *farces-attrapes* of Bergère. Sartre claimed that surrealist painting and sculpture have this breaking down of objectivity as their sole goal, that Dali's *critique-paranoïa* is a perfecting of the process to discredit reality, that surrealist literature does the same thing to language by "des télescopages de mots." (223) So the objective, destroyed by these techniques,

> renvoie soudain au subjectif, puisqu'on disqualifie la réalité et qu'on se plaît à "tenir les images même du monde extérieur pour instables et transitoires" et à "les mettre au service de la réalité de notre esprit." Mais le subjectif s'effondre à son tour et

laisse paraître, derrière lui, une mystérieuse objectivité. Tout cela sans qu'une seule
destruction réelle ait été seulement amorcée. (233)

There are several difficulties with these statements, one of which
Sartre himself brought up a few pages later: Breton never intended really
to destroy objects physically. Sartre quoted him from 1925, writing that
the immediate reality of the surrealist revolution is not so much to change
"l'ordre physique et apparent des choses que de créer un mouvement
dans les esprits." (225) In fairness to Breton also, it must be pointed out
that in 1925 the surrealists were struggling to figure out what they believed, that Breton was uncertain of what course to take vis-à-vis the
Communist Party, and that the surrealists simply were not up to producing such a complete and rigorously intellectual definition of their movement as we find in Sartre's formal philosophical works. The uncertainty
of the school's development and its internal quarrels make it fairly easy
to find contradictions.

But a greater difficulty lies in Sartre's definition of the *objet surréaliste*, on the negative aspect of which he dwelled so often. For it was
more than just a destruction of a bourgeois "objectivity," it was also a
vision or a key to the vision of that point where things cease to be considered as opposites. It is perhaps true that they were imaginary objects,
but Sartre used the word "imaginary" in a pejorative way. Nor were they
always imaginary, for they were directly related to Marcel Duchamp's
ready-mades of the dadaist period. Neither was the ready-made a physical
destruction of an existing object, but it was an existing object, not an
imaginary object. It was rather a re-perception of an existing object, a
choice to perceive an existing object in a particular way which was considered just as valid as the original "utilitarian" perception.

The best-known ready-made is probably the urinal which Duchamp
submitted to an exhibition under the title "Fontaine." When it was rejected on grounds that it was immoral, plagiarized, and that it was a piece
of plumbing, Duchamp defended himself by saying that whether Mr. Mutt
made the fountain with his own hands was without importance. "Il l'a
choisie. Il a pris un élément ordinaire de l'existence et l'a disposé de telle
sorte que la signification utilitaire disparaisse sous le nouveau titre et le
nouveau point de vue—il a créé une pensée nouvelle pour cet objet."[56]

"Tout cela sans qu'une seule destruction réelle ait été seulement
amorcée," we quoted Sartre. But then the surrealist never intended to
destroy the object because (and this is the principal point of the discussion) in surrealism the object and consciousness are related, even inter-
dependent concepts. They were the two concepts, which we may
generalize as self and nonself, which were to be united, which were to be

perceived as noncontradictory. For the surrealist, the world was unthinkable without the presence of man, and it makes no sense to discuss the object in itself, as it "really" is in the absence of man. I do not believe that a primordial "univers objectif" ever occurred to him. The world of the surrealist was a world where man was eminently present, and accompanied by objects. What he wanted to do with this state of affairs, however, was quite different from what Sartre would do with it, as we shall see when we consider *La Nausée*.

The object was only important for the surrealist as it was perceived, and the *objet surréaliste* is the artistic, or poetic, expression of this perception, of the relation of the consciousness to objects. That is why the urinal may be perceived as a fountain. The surrealist was not a platonist, nor an essentialist. If he had been, the object would have preserved its identity. The surrealist is not concerned with noumena or essences.

Breton defended himself against charges of idealism in the *Second manifeste* as well as against materialism. The rose is successively that one which comes from the garden,

> celle qui tient une place singulière dans un rêve, celle impossible à distraire du "bouquet optique," celle qui peut changer totalement de propriétés en passant dans l'écriture automatique, celle qui n'a plus que ce que le peintre a bien voulu qu'elle garde de la rose dans un tableau surréaliste, et enfin celle, toute différente d'elle-même, qui retourne au jardin. Il y a loin de là, à une vue idéaliste quelconque. . . .[57]

At the same time he denies that as a surrealiste he can be considered a traditional materialist by those conservatives who have "aucun désir de tirer au clair les relations de la pensée et de la matière." If he can be accused of materialism, it is of the Engels variety, defined as "une *intuition du monde* appelée à s'éprouver et à se réaliser."[58]

The *objet surréaliste* then becomes a meeting of man and the object, a thing that could not exist without the man, a mixing and a coalescing of human consciousness and the object. The *objet surréaliste* is a phenomenon par excellence—even if only in an aesthetic way, as a symbol, a key, or a mandala,[59] but its function was to break down the barriers of perception that separated man from the object as a concrete, stable identity in the external world, which was to break down the existence of the object as ideal.

If this sounds exaggerated, we should remember that the highly Oriental overtones of surrealism (e.g., the point where things cease to be perceived as opposites) are a very real reaction against a platonic dualism. Platonism for the surrealist was, in effect, the mode of bourgeois perception, willing to study the existence of things in the absence of man; moreover, it is the kind of mentality that gives the possibility of the *esprit du sérieux*, wherein rights become things that one can possess. Sartre did not question that these things exist in the absence of man, that they have a separate existence, but that existence is not relevant to the phenomenologist, just as it is not relevant for the surrealist. Platonism studies the ideal, the noumenon, in effect. The definition of phenomenon demands the presence of perception, and the freedom of perception the surrealist demands allows him to call a urinal a fountain. If the surrealist were an essentialist he would not be able or allowed to see anything but the aspects of the ideal. When we look at an *objet surréaliste*, we see a perception, we see man's consciousness as much as the object, and we really do break through to a greater reality. However, this greater reality, of an aesthetic nature probably, is of little interest to the proletariat and is not always accessible to it. That does not make it invalid, but from a Marxist attitude toward objects makes it practically immoral, as we shall see at the end of this section.

I would not want to insist that the surrealist was a phenomenologist, but he had nothing to do with the so-called fixed and substantial natures of things, with their true or ideal being, the ontal world of permanent being, or the world of permanent truth. Thus there is a similarity in the worlds of Sartre and the surrealist, because they are both concerned with a total picture of man and his relation to things, whether they consider that man separates himself from things by *néantisation* (by rejecting being, thereby becoming a *pour-soi* and maintaining his subjectivity by this separation), or, whether he can destroy that distance between himself and objects and achieve a state of noncontradiction which is, in effect, similar in nature to that mysterious point in alchemy,[60] or the enlightenment characteristic of several Oriental philosophies.

In both cases, Sartrean and surreal, we begin with two concepts: man and the world of objects. Both will admit that there are relations between the two concepts (e.g., the *pour-soi* is rooted in the *en-soi*, that is its facticity); but the surrealist tries to bring the concepts together into a unity, whereas Sartre denies that this unity is possible, and would reject it anyway because it would let the *pour-soi* founder in a primitive indifferentiation.

We began this discussion with Sartre's assertion that the surrealist was trying to destroy objectivity, and that he had, in effect, destroyed nothing. We have tried to demonstrate that for the surrealist it was not a question of simply destroying objectivity, but of creating something else; not of destroying the external world at all, but of destroying the simplistic relation of the consciousness to it, and of altering that relation.

This discussion of destruction leads us directly to our next problem. Not only had the surrealists destroyed nothing, continued Sartre, quite the contrary happened. By means of symbolic annulation of the ego by automatism, of objects by producing evanescent objectivity, of language by producing aberrant meanings,

> de la destruction de la peinture par la peinture et de la littérature par la littérature, le surréalisme poursuit cette curieuse entreprise de réaliser le néant par trop plein d'être. C'est toujours en *créant*, c'est-à-dire en ajoutant des tableaux aux tableaux déjà existants et des livres aux livres déjà édités, qu'il détruit. (223)

There are three major points to be made from this quotation: (1) that Sartre admitted that the surrealist movement was just as creative as it was destructive, whereas he was pleased to emphasize the destructive aspect in this essay. By its very attempt to destroy, it created. (2) The phrase which describes what surrealism was apparently trying to do (réaliser le néant par trop plein d'être) is a particular Sartrean ontological expression which can very doubtfully be applied to the situation in question. (3) The whole quotation does not accurately describe what did take place: what did occur should be described in terms of art versus research, of literature versus revolution, and was, in fact, not so greatly different from Sartre's own problem of the *engagement* of prose, but not of poetry.

If we consider what Breton was trying to do, and what Sartre described him as trying to do, we will see that they are different. To destroy literature by literature was precisely what Breton was not trying to do— he was trying to destroy *some* literature by surrealist activity. Sartre used the word literature here to mean almost anything that is written. Breton used the word to mean that written creative expression where artistic and esthetic considerations are the basic concern. The often-quoted definition of surrealism from the *Premier manifeste* specifically prohibits esthetics ("en dehors de toute considération esthétique") from surrealist activity, and practically all the purges carried out by Breton were the result of literary activity on the part of the member excommunicated. Artaud was ejected because he wanted to be an actor. *L'Immaculée conception* was not intended to be a book of poems; it was surrealist research carried out by the technique of automatism. *Nadja* was not a novel, it was a report on a woman who led a surreal existence.

As we look back on the interwar years, we are obviously going to call surrealist writing by the general term of literature, but if we express their intentions by saying they were trying to destroy literature by literature, to create nothingness by a plenum of being, we are willingly obscuring the real issue, and making the surrealists look a little ridiculous.

As late as 1939, discussing the recent additions to the movement (Matta, Paalen, etc.), Breton did not speak of surrealist art, rather of surrealist painting, and emphasized the new mechanical techniques for producing paintings that insured automatism.[61] Paalen's effort, inspired by the ideas of Einstein, to transfer the concept of time into a visual fourth dimension was described as research. But by this time it appears that Breton was too concerned about maintaining the strength and influence of the movement to indulge in any more purges—except for Avida Dollars (Salvador Dali). He willingly consorted with artists. "C'est en somme à partir de ce moment, . . . où Breton se range, qu'il le veuille ou non, dans la catégorie des *artistes*, que nous daterions l'avortement du mouvement surréaliste."[62] Surrealism has succeeded as a major movement in modern art and literature to the extent, ironically, that its adherents deviated from Breton's anti-esthetic orthodoxy. This problem of avoiding the reduction of surrealist activity to art is related directly to the problem we must presently discuss of the divorce between the artist and the proletariat, and is the same problem as allowing a revolutionary movement to "degenerate" into a literary movement, thereby being rendered innocuous.

A case can be made that surrealism and existentialism are not basically literary movements in their intent, although their expression is mainly in art and literature, and their intuitions are accessible through literature. Their goals are not the production of a body of art and literature which would add to man's culture (although it does), but the goal was a change in culture—whether on the level of the mind or in the socioeconomic sphere. The trouble is that both have recognized that a proper revolution must include both the spiritual and socioeconomic aspects, and the question of priorities was almost insurmountable. The revolution in men's minds demands different techniques and different kinds of men to implement them than the social revolution, and these different kinds of men may very well find compatibility difficult. It is quite understandable that Sartre would feel more distrust for a movement which made claims to revolution but did not bring it about than toward a merely literary movement.

Obviously, neither Sartre nor Breton rejected poetry as a valid esthetic endeavor, but the purely esthetic does not contribute to the purpose at hand. Breton believed that the artistic aspect of surrealism could not justify it. And Sartre did not believe that poetry can be *engagé*, by definition, and opted personally for prose, again as if a purely esthetic effort was not justifiable on grounds of action or *engagement*. Naturally Breton objected strongly to reducing an activity defined as seeking the point where things ceased to be perceived as contradictory to a technique for creating saleable books and paintings. One can well imagine Sartre's reaction to any effort to turn the attitudes of existentialism into a literary movement! How could one take a philosophy whose intent was the realization, assumption, and commitment of freedom and apply it to the production of plays, novels, and poems as its basic reason for being!

Breton, by refusing the estheticization of surrealism was showing a concern similar to Sartre's, that a revolutionary movement (whether in men's minds or in society) should be turned into an artistic movement, thereby becoming acceptable to the bourgeoisie, and rendered innocuous. A revolution accepted by the bourgeoisie is no longer a revolution, so Breton purged those he suspected of using surrealism to make a living. As long as it was not art, it was revolutionary.

And vice versa, as long as it was art it was not revolutionary. Breton tried rather ineffectively, I believe, to make this point work in favor of Aragon when he defended his "Front Rouge" against charges that it incited to violence. Thus, "Descendons les flics camarades," as part of the total poem, should be judged on its "pouvoir d'incarnation d'une idée," and is not necessarily revolutionary. We have a similar problem with Sartre's judgment that poetry is not *engagé* by definition, when we consider such a thing as Eluard's "Liberté."

Art has a way of being accepted, becoming respectable. Sartre tried to save himself from the same trap by refusing the Nobel prize for literature in 1964. "J'aurais été récupéré," the papers quoted him. A man who accepts such a prize as an individual, "même s'il a des opinions 'extrêmes,' on le récupère nécessairement, d'une certaine façon, en le couronnant. C'est une manière de dire: Finalement, il est des nôtres. Je ne pouvais pas accepter ça." The paradox was, he continued, that by refusing the prize, I did nothing. "C'était en l'acceptant que j'aurais fait quelque chose, que je me serais laissé récupérer par le système."[63] But in spite of his refusal, Sartre probably was caught, made "respectable" in other men's eyes, for that is the irony of the writer's relation to society. By refusing the prize, he became even more acceptable to a public that prizes such character, and such lofty reasons. His name is still in the list of Nobel Prize winners, even if "refused" is added after his name.

The finest example of antisocial, unrepentant behavior being reduced to literature and accepted is the work of Genêt. His plays, some of which are private masturbation dreams, are attended and seriously considered by businessmen, politicians, not to mention professors. His horrible subjects have, ironically, been intellectualized by Sartre in *Saint Genêt*, and have therefore become intellectually digestible, even while Sartre is telling us they should not be. In the last chapter of that book, Sartre tells us that we must be shocked, naively indignant, that this material is meant to shock and we should be shocked. The trap that Genêt catches us in is that we seek to and do understand him, and are therefore reduced to his level. But this trick works against both parties, for Genêt understood is Genêt intellectualized; he is also raised to our level, and his work becomes art. We pay him for his plays and books, he becomes *récupéré*, inadvertently joins the bourgeoisie. He then becomes similar to the pre-World War I authors Sartre describes in *Littérature*, (212) where the divorce between author and public lies only in the heart of the author. We see the same attempt to "récupérer" an artist in 1972 when General Franco is trying to get Picasso to put "Guernica" in the Prado, or when the Chamber of Commerce of Sauk Center, Minnesota, renames its principal thoroughfare "The Original Main Street" and opens a Sinclair Lewis museum.

Sartre continued his consideration of surrealist destruction with the assertion that the surrealist's works are ambivalent: they are necessarily contributions to culture, and at the same time a "projet d'anéantir tout le réel en s'anéantissant avec lui." As a result of this ambivalence "le Néant chatoie à sa surface. . . ." (224) We have seen that the writer is pretty well trapped into making contributions to his culture but it was not the surrealist's plan to "anéantir le réel" or himself except as a preparation for the *surréel*. Sartre is describing dadaism, which admittedly had a strong admixture of nihilism.

He next attacks the reason for this destruction, quoting the surrealists themselves to the effect that contributing to the instability of the images in the external world was in order to put them "au service de la réalité de notre esprit." (223) But Sartre found this spirit elusive; it is only glimpsed fluttering about through the accumulation of self-destructive objects, in this *néant* that sparkles on the surface as a result of surrealist activity. What is this *néant*? Not Hegelian negativity, nor hypostasized Negation, nor even *le Néant*, although it comes close to it. He called it *l'Impossible*. When we come to a consideration of the unification of opposites in the second part of this study, we will see that he qualified the union of the *en-soi* and *pour-soi* the same way in *l'Etre et le Néant*. It is the same *Impossible* Sartre described as being that toward which the *pour-soi* transcends itself. It is the *Impossible*, or, he wrote, almost quoting from the *Second manifeste*, "le point imaginaire où se confondent le songe et la veille, le réel et le fictif, l'objectif et le subjectif." (224) He condemned it as being confusion and not synthesis:

> car la synthèse apparaîtrait comme une existence articulée, dominant et gouvernant ses contradictions internes. Mais le surréalisme ne souhaite pas l'apparition de cette nouveauté qu'il faudrait contester encore. Il veut se maintenir dans l'énervante tension que provoque la recherche d'une intuition irréalisable. (224)

The remarks in this quotation are hard to accept, for who is to say if such a unification is synthesis or confusion, and just how the opposites operate within this unity? For the surrealist description of unification as the ideal in the *Second manifeste* is in essence the same ideal as that of several Oriental religions and philosophies, and is an experience variously described by Western theologians as "natural mysticism" as opposed to religious or Catholic mysticism.[64] Whether one is willing to accept this intuition as *irréalisable* or not depends on one's own beliefs and criteria of proof. It remains true that many philosophies and religions have considered this intuition to be attainable, which in itself is no proof, but it does appear to be a state that is experienceable, even if not observable from the outside. (For a discussion of empirical evidence of the existence of Nirvana, see F. C. Northrop, "The Undifferentiated Aesthetic Continuum," *Philosophy East and West*, April, 1964.) But the last two sentences in the above quotation are hardest to understand because in them Sartre simply asserted that the surrealists did not really want to do what they said they did, that they did not want the unification, that they wanted to remain in a state of tension. This is an accusation of bad faith for which there is no answer. Sartre then continued more in the manner of a satire than an analytic essay:

> Du moins Rimbaud voulait-il voir un salon dans un lac. Le surréaliste veut être perpétuellement sur le point de voir lac et salon: si d'aventure, il les rencontre, il s'en dégoûte ou bien il prend peur et va se coucher. Pour finir il fait beaucoup de peinture et noircit beaucoup de paper, mais il ne détruit jamais rien pour de vrai. (224)

What Rimbaud did is not particularly relevant. Although he can be claimed as an ancestor of surrealism with his "dérèglement de tous les sens," he did not emphasize any intuition of unification, and the comparison of the surrealist ideal with his pronouncement does not prove anything. It is probably unfair to Sartre to criticize him for his evaluation of the movement in 1947, from our vantage point in 1981. Although the surrealists did not destroy culture, or turn libraries into ashes, they did much to destroy the sanctity of the art object; to make humor respectable in the context of serious art; to introduce chance into art and make it acceptable; to give the *coup de grâce* to the classic concept of the necessity of discipline to overcome difficulty as the key to the creative process; and put the word "surreal" into the common man's vocabulary to mean an acceptable use of the weird or illogical. Their efforts have undoubtedly lowered the common man's threshold of acceptance for the illogical, raised his level of tolerance for the nonrational in art, advertising, entertainment, and life-style, and struck an underhanded blow at respect for reason and the utilitarian on every level. Even dada is still alive, according to Hans Richter, in the "happening," which he calls "neo-dada."[65]

All this destruction which destroyed nothing, continued Sartre, is similar to what has always been called "conversion philosophique." (225) The world, annihilated without being touched, has simply been "mis entre parenthèses." The surrealist painting, etc., is "la réalisation manuelle des aphories par lesquelles les sceptiques du IIIe siècle avant J.-C. justifiaient leur "εποχη" perpetuelle." Then Carneades and Philo could go ahead and live happily in a world miraculously preserved by its destruction. The surrealists do the same thing, he writes. They could love the world, its women, its flowers, haunted by the impossible and nothingness: that is what is called "le merveilleux surréaliste," and is that *merveilleux* of *le Grand Meaulnes* radicalized. We saw the *merveilleux surréaliste* in Bergère.

Carneades the sceptic, according to Clitomachus, was supposed to have said:

> We sceptics follow in practice the way of the world, but without holding any opinion about it. We speak of the Gods as existing and offer worship to the Gods and say that they exercise providence, but in saying this we express no belief, and avoid the rashness of the dogmatisers.[66]

Carneades meant to demonstrate that the sceptics' behavior was orthodox, even if they could not prove, for example, the existence of God. There is not a great difference between this type of reasoning and the "morale provisoire" of Descartes, which allowed him to go on functioning as a normal citizen before his final proofs were in. But Sartre uses Carneades to attack the surrealists as practicing one thing and believing another. His main reason for this attack is, as we shall presently see, the particular brand of Marxist literary history he is pursuing in *Littérature*.

If the surrealists had proclaimed social revolution as their primary concern, they then could be accused of not doing as they believed. Since their basic concern was surrealist activity and the revolution in men's minds, we would have to look at the lives of Breton, Eluard, Soupault, Péret, Crevel, etc., etc., to see if their actions corresponded with their beliefs, before we could accuse them of putting the world "entre parenthèses."

Sartre, in effect, accuses the surrealists of enjoying the world and its objects, all the while recognizing despair, the absurd, and the exploitation of the proletariat; it is as if it would be more proper for them not to give the appearance of enjoying themselves so much, not to let themselves go "sans vergogne à leur immense amour du monde." (225)

Writers on surrealism frequently do not emphasize the idea of a surrealist despair, but it is there at the basis of their preoccupation with suicide. "Qui leur fera FINALEMENT entendre qu'il n'y a pas d'espoir, qu'il n'y a rien à attendre, que c'est comme ça, qu'ils sont des autruches, des avortons, des monstres, . . .'' writes Aragon. "Qu'on me donne le haut-parleur pour que mon cri au loin s'entende. . . . Il n'y a de paradis d'aucune espèce.''[67] "Nous sommes dans une impasse, comment sortir de cette impasse, une terrible impasse.''[68] And in his discussion of suicide: "Comme s'il y avait des raisons de vivre.''[69] It is perhaps true that the surrealists never got to the other side of that despair where life begins, and that their activity was an attempt at evasion. For Aragon there was no hope, and no way out of despair; humor itself denied solutions to the problem, but it was a defense mechanism.

It should be pointed out that the apparent enthusiasm of the "merveilleux surréaliste" is not due to ignorance of the human condition, nor is it an intellectual trick whereby one may put it "entre parenthèses," but that there is a very real substratum of despair in it. The humor of the surrealists was *humour noir*. And there is no contradiction in loving the world "avec ses arbres et ses toits, ses femmes, ses coquillages, ses fleurs" (225) and knowing the anguish of the human condition. In fact, that helps to put the anguish into it. Loving that "monde de tous les jours" (225) is perhaps a basic cause of despair. The problem with Sartre is that he does not see humor as playing any role in man's relation to the external world, in man's condition. This is not to say that there is not a wry humor in "L'Enfance," or in "Erostrate," or that Sartre has no sense of humor. But humor as a tool in the fight against absurdity is simply not accepted: man's situation is pretty grim, and the Sartrean man faces it in a businesslike manner. Although he is not a depressed figure, beating his breast in despair, wallowing in pessimism, or sinking into a quiet stoicism, his struggle for authenticity has a certain stern and sober character which leaves no place for a dark humor. The Sartrean hero does not indulge in any shenanigans for the sake of striking out at absurdity or astonishing the bourgeoisie—rather he fires on the approaching Germans from a tower (*Mort dans l'âme*), kills a dissenter and assumes his proper role as leader in the revolution (*le Diable et le bon Dieu*), or kills his mother and takes his place in the world (*Les Mouches*) etc.

Now Sartre makes the point he has been leading up to in this discussion of surrealist destruction-nondestruction, and connects the surrealists to his major theme of the divorce between the writer and the ruling classes, or the writer as revolutionary. Certainly, he writes, their passion was sincere, as was their hate of the bourgeoisie. "Seulement la situation n'a pas changé: il faut se sauver sans faire de casse—ou par une casse symbolique—se laver de la souillure originelle sans renoncer aux avantages de sa position." (226) And by what follows, we see that it is not simply a question of renouncing bourgeois values because they are shallow and unauthentic, but of coming into contact with the working class and contributing to the revolution of the proletariat. Basically, he continues, the surrealists counted on their radical, metaphysical destruction to confer on them a dignity superior to that of the parasitic aristocracy (i.e., parasitic on the working classes). They were not trying to escape the bourgeoisie, but the human condition.

This last statement contains in germ the whole problem, and that problem is that escaping the bourgeoisie and escaping the human condition are two different things. For escaping from the bourgeoisie here means for Sartre the writer's escape from bourgeois values and finding a public in the working class, therefore fulfilling the writer's Marxist commitment to the destruction of class distinctions. But escaping from the human condition is an individual problem, on the individual level rather than on the social level. However, Sartre did not emphasize that difference here because he was busy with the surrealists. His *Critique de la raison dialectique* was however, an explicit admission that dialectical materialism does not sufficiently take into account the individual human experience. Sartre properly remarked that the surrealists were not simply attacking the family patrimony, but the world itself. But when he said that it was not sufficient for them to be the parasites of the bourgeoisie (as the symbolists and pre-World War I writers were described in the first part of "Situation de l'écrivain en 1947") but that "ils ont ambitionné d'être ceux de l'espèce humaine," (226) he then was returning to satire; for the parasitism of the traditional artist on the bourgeoisie, and the so-called parasitism of the surrealist on the human race are not commensurable entities, and just how the surrealist is a parasite on the human race is not clear.

Sartre condemned the surrealist escape from the bourgeoisie: "Il est clair que leur déclassement s'est fait par en haut et que leurs préoccupations leur interdisaient rigoureusement de trouver un public dans la classe ouvrière." (227) This statement is quite true, but it should not necessarily be used to condemn the surrealists alone, (except as the surrealists, different from any preceding artistic movement, proclaimed an interest in social revolution). Literary movements in France, particularly since Symbolism, have typically appealed to an intellectual aristocracy, and have almost without exception been inaccessible to the working class. Surrealism *and* existentialism are no exception. The condemnation of this "déclassement d'en haut" implies that the way to the working class is a simplification of content, a democratization of literature and art which Sartre himself never practiced. Few major artists would produce specifically for the proletariat.

Just as a man who is alienated from society, but who produces art, is absorbed into that society (as we remarked in the case of Genêt), so also a man who produces art, particularly profound art, finds himself cut off from the working classes to a great extent. That is not the way it should be, perhaps, nor the way it has to be, but a man who has to spend most of his life in a factory just to earn a living for himself and his family does not have time to get the education or to spend time trying to understand Mallarmé, or Tanguy, or Sartre. That we should produce art he could appreciate by making it easily digestible does not appear to be acceptable.

Breton did not deny that there was a divorce between the artist and the worker, and he admitted that he did not know what to do about it. He remarked that there was a certain divorce "entre l'artiste et l'ouvrier combattant tous deux de la même armée révolutionnaire."[70] The artist benefits from bourgeois culture and finds himself in a secret adventure, listening to the inner voice of the poet. The danger is that this voice may drown out all others.

Sartre found a statement of the problem in Breton's remark "Transformer le monde, a dit Marx. Changer la vie, a dit Rimbaud. Ces deux mots d'ordre pour nous ne font qu'un." (227) He believed this was cloudy thinking, and in it he saw the bourgeois intellectual disqualified, "Car il s'agit de savoir quel changement précède l'autre." (227) The Marxist does not doubt that social change must precede modifications in thought and feeling, he continued, and taxes Breton with the charges leveled against Epictetus (another stoic) by the revolutionaries, to the effect that the stoic duality between external and internal would allow a man to be free even in chains, as long as his thoughts were his own. Now Sartre put Breton on the side of the stoics, whereas shortly before this, as we have noted, he said Breton had destroyed the basis for the stoic's morality.

Sartre reduced the divorce of the artist and the worker to the absurd, because obviously it was not a question for Breton of justifying slavery or learning how to be free in chains. Nor was it a question of failing to adhere to the ideals of the social revolution: it was a question of joining the Communist party and submitting to its intransigeance. If we gave a thumbnail sketch of the movement, we would see that surrealism as a spiritual revolution attempted to concern itself with politics. But surrealists would participate in the revolution as surrealists, not as Communists. However, the party demanded all their energy and devotion for the political aspect. Thus their refusal to commit suicide got them ejected from the party. Sartre himself was not willing to submit to that kind of narrow discipline.

Perhaps the surrealists tried to do too much at once, "en amalgamant les intérêts de l'esprit et ceux de la classe ouvrière,"[71] by trying to be a specialized part of the Revolution and leaving the political aspects to the Communists. Sartre denies that Breton's remark about Marx and Rimbaud (quoted above) implies any "métamorphose progressive et connexe de l'état social et de la vie intime," (227) and quotes Breton's definition of surrealism[72] to prove that the surrealists are not only divorced from the bourgeoisie, as they wanted to be, but by that same token, much more separated from the working class. This definition is used to demonstrate that surrealism is highly remote from the working class which needs to distinguish the real from the imaginary in order to bring about its goals. This is undoubtedly true, but a more appropriate criticism of this particular definition should point out that this esoteric point of non-contradiction Breton mentions is a non-Western ideal of unification of opposites which tends not to isolate the object in the external world, thus not contributing toward technological advancement. It is thus not at all an effective attitude for an industrial society, and is a realization that is best attained by monks after years of meditation in a hut in the mountains. Sartre, however, used it to emphasize the divorce between surrealism and the proletariat, and the separation of inner values and social action. He had just stated that the problem is one of priorites (quoted earlier), i.e., of which change precedes the other, but later in the essay he denied that they are separate:

> Il faut donc apprendre simultanément aux uns que le règne des fins ne se peut réaliser sans Révolution et aux autres que la Révolution n'est concevable que si elle prépare le règne des fins. C'est cette perpétuelle tension, si nous pouvons y tenir, qui réalisera l'unité de notre public. En un mot, nous devons dans nos écrits militer en faveur de la liberté de la personne *et* de la révolution socialiste. On a souvent prétendu qu'elles n'étaient pas conciliables: c'est notre affaire de montrer inlassablement qu'elles s'impliquent l'une l'autre. (332)

The conclusion here is that both Breton and Sartre have realized that the revolution has two aspects, individual and social, and that posing the problem of priorities may be an artificial approach to a particular situation which cannot be dichotomized. Nevertheless, Sartre took advantage of the problem of priorities ("Car il s'agit de savoir quel changement précède l'autre") to accuse the surrealists of rejecting action, i.e., if one accepts surrealism, one refuses social action. This is the object of our next consideration.

The opposites mentioned in the above definition of surrealism are all categories of action, said Sartre, categories that the Revolution needs:

> Et le surréalisme, de même qu'il a radicalisé la négation de l'utile pour la transformer en refus du projet et de la vie consciente, radicalise la vieille revendication littéraire de la gratuité pour en faire un refus de l'action par la destruction de ses catégories. (228)

It is hardly fair or accurate to make the surrealists negate the useful and claim gratuity for art with the intention of destroying the reason for action. If the surrealists who remained around Breton can be accused of anything it is of cloudy thinking, and, at worst, cowardice. But they certainly believed in adherence to the principles of the socialist revolution. They were caught between the cultivation of spiritual values and social action, and their techniques and intellectualism were not available to the workers even if the latter had had time to indulge in them.

If the surrealists negated the useful it was because their priorities were different, and if they took up the literary claim of gratuity it was because they distrusted literature (or surrealist activity) being reduced to propaganda. They struggled with the problem of priorities and these problems split the movement several times. If they are to be accused of avoiding social action, it is basically that they refused to work within the narrow lines of official communism. There are a lot of problems which remain unanswered here: Would Aragon, who joined the party and presumably attained orthodoxy in the work toward the Revolution, be included in the above indictment? Or would he still remain a surrealist in spite of his excommunication by Breton? Are these criticisms aimed at the men themselves, or at the philosophical assumptions? Should we study their biographies or should we analyze the logical implications of the "philosophy" of surrealism? Can we separate the surrealists from surrealism in the Sartrean evaluation?

Sartre saw two results of this negation of action: quietism and permanent violence. Quietism because it made concerted, planned action impossible; and violence because it follows that any action would be sporadic, reduced to the immediate. He equated such action then with the Gidian *acte gratuit*, characterized by its immediacy. But surrealist action is not the *acte gratuit*, which is a personal act, committed without a reason or hope of profit, "l'acte désintéressé; né de soi; l'acte aussi sans but, donc sans maître; l'acte libre; l'acte autochtone."[73] But certainly surrealist action has a reason, and highly revolutionary and social overtones, even if it turns out to be embarrassing and ridiculous, and is different from that personal and very private affirmation of liberty of Gide's Lafcadio pushing Fleurissoire from the train. The letter of Sadoul and Caupenne in 1930 to the valedictorian of Saint-Cyr, calling on him to resign or face a public whipping, (provoking a jail sentence and a public apology) was embarrassing, but not *gratuit*. And even Paul Hilbert's fiasco had stated reasons.

That above definition of the goal of surrealism, which Sartre used to accuse the surrealists of anti-action, brings up the point which occidentals usually seize on to accuse some Eastern philosophies of quiescence, or resignation in the face of misfortune. In fact, Buddhism did teach that life was evil, that its teachings and techniques might permit a man to step off the wheel of life and death, escaping once and for all. The surrealists were successful to the extent that they used this idea of uni- fication to seek a new vision of man's reality in the world, and influential to the extent that they failed to achieve such a Nirvana.

"Il y a du quiétisme dans tout parasitisme," continued Sartre. (228) But this accusation does not single out surrealism, for he had written earlier that intellectuals "sont nécessairement les parasites des classes ou des races qui oppriment," (100) and that they are parasites who go "à l'encontre des intérêts de ceux qui les font vivre." (105) The artist is then a parasite on the bourgeois, and both presumably parasites on the pro- letariat. Sartre's concern was that the artist come into closer contact with the workers; the surrealist tried to do this by courting the Communists. That the intellectual is a parasite, with tendencies toward quietism, was one of the reasons Sartre's preoccupations became less and less esthetic, and more and more social, for he did not want to fall into the same trap. But he did not approve of the surrealists' reasons for concerning them- selves with the revolutionary movement:

> . . . ces écrivains, qui sont aussi des jeunes gens, veulent surtout anéantir leur famille,
> l'oncle général, le cousin curé, comme Baudelaire, en 48, voyait dans la révolution
> de février, l'occasion d'incendier la maison du général Aupick; ils ont aussi certains
> complexes à liquider, l'envie, la peur. . . . (229)

He then mentioned their reaction against the war, censorship, propa- ganda, colonialism and the war in Morocco. But it was not very generous of him to emphasize that surrealist concern for social activism was due to complexes and resentment toward a figure of authority, usually a father. In spite of the fact that man is free, the childhood reaction toward parental authority was Sartre's favorite explanation for what one does in later life—as he mentioned here in the case of Baudelaire. Sartre's *Baudelaire* was a warming-up exercise for *Saint Genêt*, where we see similar expla- nations, and an entire long chapter was devoted to Flaubert's father and his influence in *L'Idiot de la famille*. One cannot help but recall from *Les Mots*:

> Il n'y a pas de bon père, c'est la règle; qu'on n'en tienne pas grief aux hommes mais
> au lien de paternité qui est pourri. Faire des enfants, rien de mieux; en avoir, quelle
> iniquité! Eût-il vécu, mon père se fût couché sur moi de tout son long et m'eût
> écrasé. Par chance, il est mort en bas âge. . . .[74]

The next few pages of "Situation de l'écrivain en 1947" and a dense 10-page footnote went particularly into the surrealists' relation with the proletariat, and in an attempt to demonstrate the anti-synthesizing action of surrealism, analyzes the action of the *objet surréaliste*.

We should note carefully in what follows the criteria on which Sartre was judging surrealism—not as a literary historian would usually do, on the basis of their search and insight into the human condition, their influence on twentieth century life in general, or the success of their artistic production, but rather in the general framework of social classes and the revolution of the proletariat, on their degree of active commitment to the Communist party, their failure to create a public in the proletariat (which has never been done), on their success as a social movement, on their negativity (which he emphasized heavily to the detriment of the positive aspects of surrealism), their avowed rejection of subjectivity (which was the starting point of Sartre's philosophy), their appreciation of the *merveilleux* and the nonrational for its own sake, and their pretense to finding a synthesis of the human totality based on something other than consciousness and lucidity.

We will also note that Sartre had a tendency to refute surrealist pronouncements by carrying them to their extreme logical conclusions, and took little note of the effects of the movement on art and literature. Still, writing in 1947, he was not able to see what would happen in the next 25 years. If he had, he would very likely still not have approved. However, from Sartre's point of view immediately after World War II, one of the major prewar movements could not have appeared very attractive. In some way those prewar currents of thought must have seemed responsible for the events leading up to the war.

Why, then, did the surrealists not succeed in making the proletariat their public? Let us summarize Sartre's answer to this question: Their accumulated discontent expressed itself in a radical negation of the bourgeoisie, a negation which was, however, metaphysical and abstract. It left the world intact, in spite of some scandalous behavior. They wanted to continue their spiritual experiences, while someone else took care of the actual destruction. They wanted to be the "clercs d'une société idéale dont la fonction temporelle serait l'exercice permanent de la violence." (230)

We must point out, however, that it was the Communist party specifically whose discipline the surrealists refused to follow, and that party and discipline should hardly be referred to as an ideal society whose temporal function is the exercise of violence. It is true that the surrealists wanted to be the "spiritual" wing, so to speak, of the party; as such they can be accused of not taking any direct action, but they were not, as Sartre claimed, in the same relation to the party that the *camelots du roi* were to *l'Action française*.

He then accused the surrealists of not seeing the contradiction between a total destruction, an absolute which is a poetic fiction and harms no one, and a partial and physical destruction which is performed with a positive, general goal in mind. The surrealists simply made an absolute out of what was supposed to be a means. We may conclude from this that the proletarian revolution cannot use an absolute, which is poetic and not efficacious, and that the surrealists are effectively cut off from social action. It is undoubtedly true, as Sartre continued, that the party used the surrealists as a temporary ally, accepting their automatic writing and *hasard objectif* to disconcert the bourgeoisie, rejecting them when they were no longer needed. But that the party did this because negation is the essence of surrealism, because the surrealists were interested in the revolution as pure violence, as he affirmed, is simply an accusation of the worst kind of bad faith, and of reducing violence to an esthetic entity. The break between the Communist party and the surrealists was for a much more prosaic reason: their brand of violence and their ideas were not practically applicable, and as Breton admits in the *Second manifeste*, he simply was not able to put together a statistical report on the economic situation in Italy.

Thus, concluded Sartre, although at first it appeared that we had found that community of interest between the intellectuals and the oppressed classes which was the chance of the authors in the eighteenth century, we find that the abstractness of surrealism, and the lack of direct action on the public enthusiasm (which was the case with Diderot, Rousseau, and Voltaire on their eighteenth-century bourgeois readers) cut off any connection with the working class and force the surrealists to find their public in the intellectuals, in that bourgeoisie which they insult and of which they are the parasites. He then quoted Breton to the effect that the spiritual question is separate from the social question, that surrealism must be left free to pursue its course independent even of Marxism, but that the surrealists hope for the passage of power into the hands of the working class. (232)

We have already remarked on this division of social and spiritual and on the consequent and almost insoluble problem of priorities, and whether the problem should even be considered as one of priorities. But it is also questionable whether we can criticize the surrealists for not creating a public in the proletariat by drawing a parallel with the *philosophes* and their bourgeois public in the eighteenth century. The only relation we can make is between writer and public, for the rest of the *philosophes* of the eighteenth are not comparable to the surrealists of the twentieth century. The former stressed the rights of man, political reform, the sanctity of the individual in discursive or at most satirical literature, and in easily accessible concepts. The latter talk about esoteric and mysterious levels of consciousness, about the revolution in men's minds, and produce weird and frequently offensive poems and paintings. The eighteenth century bourgeois cannot be compared to the modern proletariat for obvious reasons, and the *philosophes* did not reach the peasants (the country working class) and probably would not have reached the proletariat if there had been one in the eighteenth century. The French Revolution was mainly a bourgeois revolution, and a proletarian revolution cannot utilize the writer's or artist's product in the same fashion.

Thus the accusation that the French Communist party, having arrived at the constructive phase of its development, turned away from surrealism because it remained "*négatif* par essence," surely does not tell the whole story. Much more just was Sartre's following summation:

> Ainsi la première tentative de l'écrivain bourgeois pour se rapprocher du prolétariat demeure utopique et abstraite parce qu'il ne cherche pas un public mais un allié, parce qu'il conserve et renforce la division du temporel et du spirituel et qu'il se maintient dans les limits d'une cléricature. (263)

Just as we were saying above, this was the first attempt to reach the proletariat, a class that consumes a different kind of literature and art. And it was precisely the failure of surrealism to reach the working class because it was presenting intangibles to a class interested mainly in tangibles.

The refusal of the surrealists to conform to party discipline and direct their action to immediately practical purposes, organization, reports, etc., was branded by Sartre as negativity made a poetic absolute, lying outside history, a negativity which is "la fin absolue de la vie et de l'art." (234) At first it is difficult to see how surrealism could be the end of life and art, but if we were to succeed in reaching the ideal of unification and the destruction of subjectivity, the character of life would change drastically; and if automatism prevailed, the creativity process would cease to exist as we know it in favor of a kind of cosmic, effortless expression. This has not happened, of course. In fact, dada-surrealism has probably been the richest source of artistic renewal in the twentieth century. But it was typical of Sartre in this essay to follow surrealist concepts to their extreme logical conclusions.

In *Littérature*, beginning particularly with the section "Pour qui écrit-on?" Sartre described several possible historical writer-public relationships: "le déclassement par en haut, le parasitisme, l'aristocratie, métaphysique de consommation et l'alliance avec les forces révolutionnaires." (234) The surrealist movement is original, he continued, in that it tried to appropriate all these categories at the same time. At least by

.

Sartre's definition, they pretty well succeeded in all but the last, which was the most important one for him. Still, he gave them credit for the first attempt at reaching the working class, but stated that it would have been impossible before that time anyway because it was the Communist party which had to play the role of mediator between an intellectual aristocracy and the oppressed. In this case, it was not only the surrealists who failed to find a proletarian public, but the party which failed to mediate. The role of the intellectual or the converted bourgeois is a thorny one for the party, and we see it cropping up in *Les Mains sales*.

As Sartre demonstrated Breton's refusal to accept Marxism and work within the Party, so also he showed that after the Second World War the break with the Communist party became definitive. (360) Surrealism lost its *actualité*, he continued, and several writers were attempting to integrate it into bourgeois humanism: Claude Mauriac sees it as an *entreprise de connaissance*, a community of spirits (although Sartre denied that the movement was ever an *entreprise de connaissance*, the *Second manifeste* stresses the research aspect of automatism which should be used to gain an understanding of the workings of the mind, and in particular the mechanics of inspiration). He quotes Bataille and Pastoureau to emphasize the break with Marxism; their pronouncements are almost exactly like those of Breton earlier, when he claimed independence to pursue the revolution in his own way, i.e., on the spiritual rather than on the socioeconomic plane. Sartre condemned this approach because at this point he had apparently opted for the priority of political action, and accused the surrealists of the opposite choice: "il est entendu, à present, qu'on peut agir sur les superstructures sans que l'infrastructure économique soit modifiée." (362) It goes without saying that this structuring of human reality into spiritual and economic strata makes some assumptions about their possible interactions that would have to be carefully investigated.

The most interesting and difficult part of this discussion is prompted by the remark of Alquié and Max Pol-Fouchet to the effect that surrealism is an attempt at liberation of the human totality. In several pages of involved and sometimes not totally clear analysis, Sartre maintained that surrealism does not contribute to a human totality because it has a strong anti-synthesizing aspect; he used the impact of the *objet surréaliste* to demonstrate that the surrealist attitude toward the object prevents an effective synthesis.

Sartre saw in Hegel the source of all the "totalizing," whether nazi, Marxist, or existentialist. We must immediately be alert to the fact that Sartre was not going to discuss surrealism on its own ground, that is, on its relative success or failure on the esthetic level to find that mysterious point of noncontradiction. The emphasis therefore will be on a synthesis as an organic unity of thesis and antithesis, and on the anti-synthetic aspects, the main one being what Sartre called "la négativité analytique qui s'exerce sur la réalité quotidienne." (363) He compared surrealist activity to Hegel's definition of scepticism: a negative attitude toward *l'être-autre*, corresponding therefore to desire and work, which destroys in thought the variety of multiplicity of the *être-autre*. But, whereas the sceptic merely destroys *en pensée*, the surrealist actively and actually goes to work on matter and destroys it. (This is a little difficult to correlate with Sartre's earlier assertion that surrealism never destroyed anything.) Therefore, for Sartre, surrealism became a "descente de l'esprit négatif dans le travail"; (363) it is sceptic negativity made concrete. Therefore the *objet surréaliste* is sceptic negativity made concrete. In our previous discussion of the *objet surréaliste*, I referred to it as spirit coming into contact with matter; here we might rephrase Sartre's statement into "spirit descending into matter."

But why did he use the qualification "négatif"? We must interpret the adjective to mean that the spirit is negating the object as it is found in the external world, i.e., it destroys it in a sense. What scepticism destroyed in idea, surrealism destroys in a material way: Sartre intended to show this by another reference to Duchamp's marble sugar-cubes. The ordinary worker, on the other hand, destroys to create: the carpenter destroys the tree to make a beam. That workman is indulging in "négativité constructrice," making use of the method of "l'analyse bourgeoise." (364) The surrealist is related to that worker in that he borrows the method but inverts it: he constructs something in order to destroy. "Cependant comme la construction est réelle et la destruction symbolique, l'objet surréaliste peut être aussi conçu comme sa propre fin." (364)

Now we come to the point I want to make from the preceding discussion: the great impact of surrealist activity, the *objet surréaliste* in particular, is that it puts us into a nonutilitarian relationship with matter. Furthermore, we have just seen Sartre make a moral judgment, accepting the workman's use of *l'analyse bourgeoise* but condemning the surrealist's perversion of it. Of the possible relationships with matter, some are to be avoided; not because they are impossible but because they are immoral. This emphasizes that Sartre was basically a moral philosopher on every level.

The negation practiced by surrealist activity is a refusal to leave the object as the naive perception found it, just as the "analyse bourgeoise" refused to leave the object alone; but in the case of the *objet surréaliste*, Sartre slipped subtly into using "négatif" and "destruction" as value judgments, to emphasize the negative aspect of surrealism—whereas there was a creative intention in the surrealist negation of a naive perception; we do not see any pejorative conotation attached to the idea of negativity in a workman's production of a beam from a tree.

The fact is that Sartre did not like nonutilitarian relationships with matter, for such relationships reveal Nature as described in the latter part of *La Nausée*, and put man in touch with it. (We will go into that in greater detail in the next section when we study unification and the impact of the object in *La Nausée*.) The *objet surréaliste* is frequently a human-ized object, but from which the humanizing aspect has been taken by surrealist activity, in particular the useful aspect (marble sugar-cubes, for example); as such the *objet surréaliste*, as Sartre said above, is creation for the purpose of destruction. Also since, according to Sartre, the *objet surréaliste* can be "conçu comme sa propre fin," it would be a thing in the world along with man but separate from him, therefore out of his control and vaguely threatening. The humanized object, on the other hand, is not for its own end, but for the end of man, its creator, and with it one may feel comfortable. Thus Sartre did not like the country, wrote Simone de Beauvoir, ". . . il ne se sent chez lui que dans les villes, au coeur d'un univers artificiel rempli d'objets fait par les hommes."[75]

Sartre's disapproval of the nonutilitarian object was consistent with his general defense of Marxism in this essay. For the materialism of Marx is not that eighteenth century variety which totally dehumanizes matter, but the "driving force is really man's relation to matter, of which the most important part is his mode of production. In this way Marx's materialism, in practice, becomes economics."[76] Sartre touched on this problem in *Baudelaire*, where he described Baudelaire's aversion to nature as being profoundly influenced by "le grand courant anti-naturaliste" which goes through the whole nineteenth century, and the production of "le rêve d'une anti-nature" brought about by the combined action of the Saint-Simonians, the positivists, and Marx.[77] The ideal Sartre defined for them and for Baudelaire might without too much injustice be applied to Sartre himself: "Il s'agit d'un ordre humain directement opposé aux erreurs, aux injustices et aux méchanismes aveugles du Monde naturel."[78] This new order is made possible, he continued, by the concept of *travail*, and particularly by *le travail industriel*; at the origins of this anti-naturalism is the industrial and mechanical revolution of the nineteenth century which caught Baudelaire in its current. Baudelaire was attracted by work, "car il est comme une pensée imprimée dans la matière. Il a toujours été tenté par l'idée que les choses sont des pensées objectivées et comme solidifiées."[79]

This idea of work is very near to that *analyse bourgeoise* of which we were just speaking, and of which the surrealist activity is the inverse.

The *analyse bourgeoise* or anti-naturalism's concept of *travail* exercises its negation on the natural object (a tree for example), destroying it in order to produce a humanized object (a beam). The inverse of this is surrealist activity which exercises its negation on the humanized object in order to produce an *objet surréaliste*, or on a natural object with the same result. This kind of radical anti-utilitarianism destroys, therefore, man's usual relationship to objects, destroys his privileged relation to them: it puts him into the world of the *en-soi* in a way the Sartrean man does not want to be, into a nontechnological relation that smacks strongly of that point at which things cease to be perceived as contradictory. This nontechnological relation to objects is one of the major characteristics of those particular Eastern philosophies that we might describe as unification-oriented, and accounts for the fact that China did not stress technological development for centuries. The development of technology requires a specific attitude toward objects, namely that in which they are perceived as specifically non-self, alien, to be controlled.

Sartre described Baudelaire's dislike of nature, of the country, of plants:

> Végétaux, légumes sanctifiés: ces deux mots marquent assez le mépris où il tient l'insignificance du monde des plantes. Il a comme une intuition profonde du monde des plantes. Il a comme une intuition profonde de cette contingence amorphe et obstinée qu'est la vie—*précisément l'envers du travail*—et il en a horreur parce qu'elle reflète à ses yeux la gratuité de sa propre conscience, qu'il veut se dissimuler à tout prix.[80]

Baudelaire came out in 1947. In it, Sartre's enthusiasm in describing Baudelaire's aversion for nature (i.e., the nonhumanized) suggested that he could almost be describing himself. In fact, Simone de Beauvoir's article from 1946 described Sartre in a similar way:

> Il déteste la campagne. Il abhorre—le mot n'est pas trop fort—la vie grouillante des insectes et la pullulation des plantes. Au plus *tolère-t-il une mer calme*, le sable régulier du désert ou le froid minéral des pics alpins; . . . Il n'aime ni les légumes crus, ni le lait qui vient d'être trait, ni les huîtres, rien que des mets cuits; et il demande toujours des fruits en conserve plutôt que le produit naturel. [My emphasis][81]

Sartre found that Baudelaire also had a "tendresse pour la mer . . . un minéral mobile,"[82] and repeatedly described him in terms that could apply to himself: "Pour lui la *vraie* eau, la *vraie* lumière, la *vraie* chaleur sont celles des villes—déjà des objets d'art";[83] in the city he was "entouré d'objets précis dont l'existence est déterminée par leur rôle et qui sont tous auréolés d'une valeur ou d'un prix . . . une réalité justifiée";[84] as for Nature, "De cette tiédeur moite, de cette abondance, il a horreur";[85]

"Cette éternité biologique lui semble insupportable";[86] "Cette énorme fécondité molle, il a surtout horreur de la sentir en soi-même."[87] He described Baudelaire's *dandysme*, his affected manners, as his dislike for abandon, for "si vous avez un humanisme de la nature, vos gestes auront une sorte de rondeur et de générosité, une aisance abandonée."[88] There is none of this *rondeur* of gesture in any of the plays of Sartre, or of that other city-dweller, Genêt, where artificiality, non-naturalness is distilled to an essence.

Jameson, in a marvelous chapter of his *Sartre*, finds a similar dehumanization working to destroy the identity of Mathieu and Paris. War has so gratuitously altered the relation of man to the city, that it has altered the city itself, transforming it from that intimate place where men live, to a network of roads. "All the gracious, the most "human" qualities of the city are gone like a mirage, mere instrumentality remains, and yet instrumentality is . . . the most human relationship of all to things."[89] Therefore the city may have been greatly dehumanized, but still is not reduced to Nature. For Nature, Jameson quotes from *Saint-Genêt*, is "Rien d'autre que le monde extérieur quand nous cessons d'avoir des relations techniques avec les choses."[90]

Thus we have seen the *objet surréaliste* destroy the utilitarian, the technological relation between man and the object, bringing him into a raw confrontation with it by means of an inverse *analyse bourgeoise*; Sartre condemned this in an essay where he attacked surrealism from the point of view of an anti-naturalist, Marxist, technologically oriented tradition. From this point of view, then, surrealism *is* anti-Marxist in its very basic activities. It bears repeating, then, that Sartre's disapproval of the nonutilitarian object was consistent with his defense of Marxism in *Littérature*.

As we have just seen, surrealist *travail* (i.e., action directed against an object with the intention of changing it, of "negating" it as it is found) is concrete destruction. So is desire, said Sartre, for desire is desire for destruction, for *consommation*. But we must point out that for the surrealists, desire was supposed to destroy the perception of the contradiction between waking and dreaming, etc., that is, it creates a unity; as love, it creates a state of grace allowing a privileged perception of reality, i.e., surreality. In Sartre's sense, then, it is negativity just as the *objet surréaliste* is, for it refuses to leave the spiritual "material" as it found it; it too tends to break down the common-sense, utilitarian, relation with the external world.

To demonstrate further that surrealism is anti-synthetic, Sartre attacked *Les Vases communicants* on the grounds that it simply demonstrates a "flux et reflux" between waking and dreaming, but that there is

no mediation and no synthetic unity. He sought the "outil de la média-
tion," adding an extra concept because he was apparently unwilling to
accept the surrealist "tools" of desire, automatism, love, abnormal mental states, madness, etc. We must assume that he was seeking a more
mechanical "tool," or question the use of the word tool in this context.
The use of tools to achieve a unity of opposites presents a thorny problem,
for what is the technique of attaining such an intuition, and how can such
a personal experience be explained. The Taoist philosophers who discussed the use of language to bring about or describe the ineffable used
the parallel of the fishnet. The word is like the net: after you have used
it to catch the fish, you lay it aside. You must use the net, but as you do
you must also realize that it is not the fish, not the end product.

If the *objet surréaliste* has succeeded in doing all Sartre said it has,
the objection that it is anti-synthetic, and as such does not contribute to
the surrealist concern to "affirmer les droits de la totalité humaine," does
not seem very telling. For as he described it, the *objet surréaliste* is
certainly a profound experience, philosophical and esthetic. At the end
of his description of it, Sartre called it *irritant*:

> Mais cet irritant chatoiement de l'impossible n'est rien au fond, sinon l'écart impos-
> sible à combler entre les deux termes d'une contradiction. Il s'agit de provoquer
> techniquement l'insatisfaction baudelairienne. Nous n'avons aucune révélation, au-
> cune intuition d'objet neuf, aucune saisie de matière ou de contenu, mais seulement
> la conscience *purement formelle* de l'esprit comme dépassement, appel et vide. (365)

These conclusions do not necessarily follow from what he has said. We
perhaps do not have any intuition of an *objet neuf*, but we do have as I
suggested earlier, an *être-là* in Sartre's terms, that dramatizes and analyzes man's relation to matter. To say that it does not put us in touch with
matter is a personal value judgment, based on a Marxian attitude toward
matter, and, we should emphasize, is a basically moral attitude.

In effect, he stated here, when we contemplate the *objet surréaliste*
we are contemplating only spirit. It seems difficult to generalize another
spectator's experience on moral grounds, and to answer for what he sees.

What Sartre was talking about here was the anti-synthesizing impact
of the *objet*, and we have just seen his reasons for that opinion. By anti-
synthesizing he meant that the object does not succeed in its intended
function of contributing to the totality of man because it is an ineffective
statement of man's relation to matter. Sartre thus said we contemplate
only the *formal* consciousness of "l'esprit comme dépassement, appel,
et vide," not any new object, "aucune saisie de matière ou de contenu."
All we do see is the "irritant chatoiement de l'impossible." Impossible
what? Impossible unity of spirit and matter, or self and nonself, etc. As

usual, Sartre maintained that this unity is impossible. As we have seen he called impossible that point where contradictions cease to exist. It is easy to dismiss the *objet surréaliste* as a failure because it does not provoke an intuition of unity or reveal the Tao in a blinding flash. (As we shall see in a later section it was not the art work which provoked the enlightenment in the Chinese artist, but the artist-sage who already knew the Tao and produced the art work by the kai-ho process.)

One is quite willing to agree with Sartre that the *objet* did not bring on a mystic union with the cosmos, but it counts for something that it can give the feeling that the artist had tried for and wanted the intuition, even if he failed. If we experience the tantalizing, "irritant" impossible, that is at least something artistically worthwhile, if not applicable to the revolution of the proletariat. Again, this "impossible," as we shall see later, is very near that intuition of totality toward which the *pour-soi* transcends itself, and indeed must transcend itself, even though it is an impossible totality.

Sartre continued with the accusation that the surrealist is a materialist because of his "amour profond de la matérialité (objet et support insondable de ses destructions)." (365) It is a little difficult to see how the surrealist could be a materialist (particularly in the eighteenth century sense) just because he practices the inverse *analyse bourgeoise* on matter, particularly when the result of this is that consciousness "fait en vérité l'expérience d'elle-même comme conscience se contredisant à l'intérieur de soi-même." (365) One could conclude just the opposite, that he hates matter, or simply that he hates only humanized matter. It does not appear advantageous to discuss the surrealist in terms of idealism or materialism.

What then does surrealism do with this consciousness, this subjectivity it has just uncovered by means of the *objet surréaliste*? (Note that Sartre had previously seemed to equate consciousness with subjectivity.) Does it, in other words, value the demonstration of that consciousness in action? No, he answered, surrealism is in love with materiality, it refuses subjectivity, covering it up with materialism, thereby avoiding that tension of subjectivity by positing an objective structure of the universe.

It is a little hard to follow Sartre here, to determine whether he was talking about the actual impact of the *objet surréaliste*, or the logical consequences of surrealism, or the contradictions in surrealist thought. He was apparently trying to deny what he said the *objet* was supposed to do for the surrealist (produce the point of noncontradiction). But this amounts to saying that what the object cannot do (unify object and subject) destroys what the object did (produce an intuition of subjectivity). This is a confrontation of surrealist theories and Sartrean explanations which is simply a confused way of approaching the problem. To restate the confusion in other terms: In the *objet surréaliste* the surrealist seeks an intuition of that point of noncontradiction where subject and object no longer exist; therefore, theoretically, the subjectivity is not supposed to exist for the surrealist. But Sartre said this does not happen; what really happens is that the *objet surréaliste* reveals a subjectivity. But then this subjectivity is refused. How can what did not happen effect what did happen? If the *objet* actually does function in one way, then it functions in that way and is not affected by what it did not do.

Naturally the artist works with matter, with objects. But how does the refusal of subjectivity make the surrealist a materialist, for he does not refuse subjectivity with the intention of explaining the universe from the material point of view as La Mettrie did. Simply because an artist has a relationship with matter does not make him a materialist, and because the *objet surréaliste* is ideally supposed to break down the barriers between spirit and matter does not mean that an explanation of the universe lies in matter, or that the *objet surréaliste* depicts an objective universe.

Let us take another objection of Sartre to the *objet surréaliste* as a failure to unify waking and dreaming: If I paint or sculpt what I saw in my dream, the waking state will then devour the dream. For this object thus created is hung on a wall, and taking its place among other objects, "devient chose du monde." (366) Therefore, a dream painted becomes a waking object, and as such is simply an addition to reality, not a synthesis. The surrealists, he continued, owe a debt to psychoanalysis because the concept of complexes provided the model for the contradictory interpretations [of reality], but they did not realize that such complexes can exist only "sur le fondement d'une réalité synthétique préalablement donnée." (366) These surrealist manifestations were simply a "collection hétéroclite" of items, and failed to liberate the totality of man because the surrealists had no idea of synthesis.

The surrealist would answer this objection by stating that the *objet surréaliste*, or the object created from a dream, was itself not the end product of surrealist activity, but that it was a piece of research, that it was supposed to provoke or stimulate the perception of unification, or noncontradiction, and to render validity to that dream world as a respectable aspect of human activity. But this objection also brings us back to the basis of Sartre's judgment: In order to replace "les unifications synthétiques qu'opère la conscience, on concevra une sorte d'unité magique, par participation, qui se manifeste capricieusement et qu'on nommera hasard objectif." (367) Sartre simply refused to accept such a magical and esoteric unification of opposites; unification for him was rather a synthesis brought about by lucid thought on the pattern of the Hegelian dialectic. He rejected the whole goal of surrealism, and accurately characterized surrealist activity as a discovery (although previously he had denied that it was an *entreprise de connaissance*). "Le surréalisme . . . a horreur des genèses et des naissances; la création n'est jamais pour lui une émanation, un passage de la puissance à l'acte, une gestation; c'est le surgissement *ex nihilo*." (367) As we have remarked, Breton emphasized this very aspect of the movement in the *Second manifeste*—surrealism is research, its productions are discoveries. "Surgissement *ex nihilo*" however is a fairly unsymphathetic way to describe surrealist activity.

If surrealist activity is merely a discovery, how could it "délivrer l'homme de ses monstres?" "Il a tué les monstres, peut-être, mais il a tué l'homme aussi." (367) Another way of stating the same thing, for it amounts to depriving man of his humanity (from a Sartrean point of view) is to see surrealism as accepting the monsters: it made man the totality of his conscious and unconscious, and as such made him a kind of monster. In some cases it nearly made him a madman who valued his madness.

The surrealists claimed they wanted to liberate human desire, charged Sartre, but forbade whole categories of desires (homosexuality, etc.) without justifying their interdiction. Furthermore, they did not study desire as such in its subjective sources, but only as it was manifested in objects (or "actes manqués, images du symbolisme onirique, etc."). Thus they are again charged with materialism. "Ce qui les passionne, ce n'est pas le désir à chaud mais le désir cristallisé, ce qu'on pourrait appeler . . . le chiffre du désir dans le monde." (367) This, I believe, was Sartre's best criticism of the surrealists, for he had, in effect, just explained why they are artists in spite of themselves. When one studies the surrealists, one often wonders why their goals of discovery and unification and their claims of research, basically a kind of psychological investigation, did not take on more the character of clinical research or of a religious practice like Zen. Breton exerted himself to fend off charges of artistry. Why then did surrealism "degenerate" into an art movement, why is it remembered as such?

Sartre had just caught them out—their interest was the production of artifacts, or *désir cristallisé*, another expression of the *analyse bourgeoise*, the descent of spirit into matter, or the confrontation of spirit and matter. This provides us the opportunity to emphasize that, if they were not psychologists, neither were they interested in matter for itself, and that if they are to be accused of materialism, then that term must be drastically redefined. Whether the "orthodox" surrealist work was art or not brings up the question of intention: can an object be called art if the creator did not mean it to be? It is similar to the question of whether rupestrian figures or the apparently ritual cave painting of primitive man are art. Whatever the answer to this question is, it is still the esthetician or art historian who considers these works. And the surrealist is not a psychologist, an idealist, or a materialist: he is basically concerned with the relationship between man and the object; he crystallizes desire in the object where he studies that relationship. Thus he produces artifacts which fall *volens nolens* into the realm of the esthetic.

In summary, Sartre tried to prove that surrealism failed in its attempt at liberation of the human totality by a lengthy consideration of the failure of the *objet surréaliste*, an object which does not contribute to a synthesis, but sometimes produces an intuition of man's subjectivity, and sometimes causes the surrealist to take refuge in materialism, according to one's point of view. Sartre's refutation was at bottom based on his belief in the impossibility of a surrealist unification; his own synthesis would have to be brought about by consciousness. His steady insistence on their rejection of subjectivity slights their ideal of a unification in which objectivity was also rejected.

He accepted, however, the contribution of surrealism to poetry, calling it the only poetic movement of the first half of the century. (368) Its value lay not in the liberation of the human totality, nor of desire however, but in the liberation of the imagination—and "l'imaginaire pur et la praxis sont difficilement compatibles." (368) He recognized the evolution of surrealism toward the acceptance of a surrealist art in the years just before and after the war, and the growing awareness in younger surrealist poets that total freedom of imagination could isolate them from other men. Such hesitations on their part would, of course, have been condemned by Breton during his period of intransigeance.

Sartre also questioned that the surrealists were acting as poets during the time they were so concerned with social action, the Communist party, and their own internal struggles. As we have seen, they were not acting as poets, but by their own standards, as surrealists, for that was a time when surrealism was an all-encompassing vision that was considered to include social action: it is hard to see that surrealism had any success in that respect. And, although Sartre conceded that a man is a unity, indivisible into politician and poet, a unity which would seem to allow the surrealist to commit himself to social action, still surrealism offers no cohesive explanation of the political man. For "il est loisible à un écrivain qui veut marquer l'unité de sa vie et de son oeuvre de montrer par une théorie la communauté de visées de sa poésie et de sa praxis." (369) Sartre himself for his own purposes seemed to have a theory that justified praxis but not art, for he almost rejected purely literary efforts for himself. He questioned whether he could read Robbe-Grillet in an underdeveloped country. And ". . . l'exploitation de l'homme par l'homme, la sous-alimentation, reléguaient au second plan le mal métaphysique, qui est un luxe . . . En face d'un enfant qui meurt, *La Nausée* ne fait pas le poids."[91] Surrealism has failed to present a unified explanation, and for this reason, explained Sartre, he attacked only the theory, couched in prose. To the accusation that he was not giving the poets credit for their contribution to "la vie intérieure," he replied that they cared little for it: "Ils voulaient la faire éclater, rompre les digues entre subjectif et objectif." (370) As usual Sartre was equating "la vie intérieure" with consciousness and subjectivity, whereas the surrealists also believed in a vast mysterious unconscious—and man was as much at its mercy as in its control. It is true that Sartre had not specifically attacked surrealist poetry, but he struck very hard at its basis, at surrealist use of language, at the function of surrealist activity in general and the *objet surréaliste* in particular; that he spared poetry shows little sympathy.

We have often remarked in this study that Sartre faced the same problem as Breton: how can one reconcile personal liberty and the fullest realization of the individual experience with a social commitment whose action is defined by Marxism and the Communist party. Sartre's evolution from *L'Etre et le Néant* and its concepts of personal freedom to *Critique de la Raison dialectique* and its emphasis on the *autrui* is the story of his effort to reconcile these two aspects. Breton seems to have given up on the problem, assuming that it was insurmountable, or at least not feeling any pressing need to explain it by a unified theory.

Albérès explains Sartre's solution as a transportation of the "dialectical movement from the collectivity to the individual and, in contrast to Marxism, sees in consciousness the source of the collectivity."[92] He quotes the *Critique* to the effect that "the whole structure of the historical dialectic rests on individual praxis insofar as it is already dialectical."[93] It is ironic that Breton said nearly the same thing in the *Second manifeste* in 1930, in reaction to the same problem:

> Le surréalisme . . . présente avec le matérialisme historique au moins cette analogie de tendance qu'il part de l' "avortement colossal" du système hégelian. Il me paraît impossible qu'on assigne des limites, celles du cadre économique par exemple, à l'exercice d'une pensée définitivement assouplie à la négation, et à la négation de la négation. Comment admettre que la méthode dialectique ne puisse s'appliquer valablement qu'à la résolution des problèmes sociaux? Toute l'ambition du surréalisme est de lui fournir des possibilités d'application nullement concurrentes dans le domaine conscient le plus immédiat.[94]

Breton never developed this idea any further, but it is basically the same tack Sartre took, adding to it the idea of *totalisation* to get from the individual to the social. Whether Sartre succeeded or not is out of the scope of this study, but it is curious that the Communist writer Roger

Garaudy levels the same accusations against Sartre that Sartre made against Breton. Whereas Doubrovsky sees in *Critique* the pure and simple abandonment of Sartre's initial positions, Garaudy finds in it the same basic mistakes as in *l'Etre et le Néant*, with which it shows a "continuité absolue."[95] In *La Nausée*, for example, he claims Sartre had mistaken the capitalist world at the peak of its decadence for the eternal human condition. "La 'nausée' n'est plus une réaction historique devant un monde qui se décompose, mais une réaction métaphysique devant la vie en général."[96] This is an accusation of nonhistoricity, which is incompatible with Marxism. Sartre, as we have seen, explained that the negativity of the Communist party was only temporary, a necessary historical moment in their attempt at social reorganization, but "la négativité surréaliste se maintient, quoi qu'on en dise, en dehors de l'histoire: à la fois dans l'instant et dans l'éternel. . . ." (233) Sartre likewise charged the surrealists with a similar metaphysical revolt, thus too abstract to reach a public in the proletariat.

Just as Sartre reproached the surrealists for refusing objectivity, Garaudy finds a similar refusal in Sartre to be one of the limits of existentialism in its initial form:

> Je suis situé dans le monde et mon point de vue sur lui sera toujours subjectif. Il y a bien, pour le sens commun comme pour la science, un monde objectif, qui est définissable comme s'il n'était vu de nulle part, mais ce n'est pas le monde de l'expérience vécue: je ne peux pas me mettre hors du monde pour l'embrasser dans sa totalité.[97]

Modern relativity rejects this concept of objectivity, "définissable comme s'il n'était vu de nulle part," and, as writers frequently point out, probably influenced the surrealist attitude toward the stability of the object. We have already discussed the nonplatonic aspect of this attitude; now Garaudy is putting Sartre in the same category because he began his philosophy with the subjective. Both Breton and Sartre had difficulty proceeding from the personal to the social, or in the terms that Garaudy uses, from the subjective to the objective world. Both Garaudy and Jeanson[98] put the Sartrean nausea in the camp of the surrealists (that problem is considered in the next section of this study). From the point of view of the doctrinaire Communist then it appears that both Breton and Sartre are guilty of the same things for the same reasons. Sartre would have difficulty accepting Garaudy's notion of objectivity by which human relations "dans des conditions déterminées de vie sociale, prennent l'apparence des choses et obéissent à des lois objectives,"[99] an objectification of human effort which avoids the abstractions of a metaphysical system. After having been so reified, human relations then become subject to manipulation.

And so, according to Garaudy, this explains why Sartre did not give Brunet a major role in *le Sursis*: he could have "objectively" explained Munich. And into the surrealist camp comes Mathieu, "à la recherche d'une liberté abstraite et vide, . . . à la surface de l'histoire comme un bout de bois mort dans un torrent."[100] When Mathieu fires on the German soldiers at the end of *Mort dans l'âme*,

> il ne cherche pas l'efficacité, mais l'exaltation: son geste n'est pas un événement social, mais un événement métaphysique et personel; sa volonté de laisser une trace de lui-même. Il n'a pas plus de signification historique que la folie d'Erostrate.[101]

Was Mathieu's act basically an *acte surréaliste*, except that it was approved by the resistance? Sartre seems to have realized this, according to Garaudy, because it explains why he did not write a fourth volume of *Les Chemins de la liberté*, i.e., that a solution is no longer valid on the individual level, but must be found in social change. Mathieu must become a Marxist, and Erostrate must become a social animal.

Sartre Visits the Surrealist Camp

Duality and Unification

Surrealism, as described by Breton in the *Second manifeste* in 1929, is an activity which seeks that point at which certain things cease to be contradictory: real and imaginary, life and death, past and future, high and low, conscious and unconscious, subjectivity and objectivity. The most general opposites are the self and nonself, in Sartrean terms the *pour-soi* and *en-soi*.

Dualism is a major characteristic of Western thought (and not all Oriental philosophies are directed toward unification), one of the basic assumptions of Platonism and Cartesianism, even though it may be expressed in varying terms, and has given rise to the so-called mind-body problem. The solution to this problem has been the concern of idealists such as Leibniz; of materialists such as Cyrano de Bergerac in the seventeenth century and La Mettrie in the eighteenth century, who in effect denied the existence of mind; of modern theologians such as Teilhard de Chardin and his law of complexity-consciousness described in *Le Phénomène humain*; and of biophysicists who measure the current across synapses in an effort to relate the concepts of physical and mental: it is a ubiquitous and perhaps the most basic question. It shows up in Valéry's "Cimetière marin," where Laurent LeSage sees a parallel with existentialism:

> Nature in "Cimetière marin" is the *en-soi* of Sartre—brute, eternal, and self-containing; man in "Le Cimetière marin" is the *pour-soi* of Sartre—anxiously aware, time-ridden, and projected outside himself. Even without forsaking the generally accepted notion that the theme of the poem is the conflict between thought and action, we can easily relate it to the Sartrean antithesis.[1]

It is typical of people dissatisfied with Occidental culture to revolt against these dualisms, and this is precisely what the surrealists were doing. It is therefore quite logical that they should have had a flirtation with Oriental philosophies, particularly with Buddhism, which purport to resolve these opposites into a greater human reality. A similar dissatisfaction shows up in the United States in the concern with Zen in the 1950s, and with the Maharishi and transcendental meditation in the 1960s and 1970s. Thus there is a parallel between surrealism and its destruction of dualities and such Oriental concepts as the Tao, the ineffable Tao, of which we may attempt a definition in Western terms as the "conscious way" wherein man becomes aware of his entire psyche, even to the level of biological continuity; or the satori, the sudden enlightenment of Zen, or in China, Ch'an Buddhism; or Nirvana; or the Bhutatathata.[2] The surrealist interest in the occult also found a similar idea in the mysterious point of alchemy discussed by Eliphas Levi in his *Histoire de la Magie*:

> Le Grand-Oeuvre, c'est la conquête du point central ou réside la force équilibrante. Partout ailleurs les réactions de la force équilibrée conservent la vie universelle par le mouvement perpétuel de la naissance et de la mort . . . Les hommes arrivés à ce point central sont les véritables adeptes, ce sont les thaumaturges de la science et de la raison . . . la nature leur obéit parce qu'ils veulent ce que veut la loi qui fait marcher la nature.[3]

It is not too surprising that automatic writing, or automatism in general, as a technique for letting the secret man speak, should have a parallel in Taoism, in the technique called the *k'ai ho*. The *k'ai ho* produces the ability, when mastered, to create poetry and paintings quickly and effortlessly due to what amounts to a destruction of the dualities in man, or to preventing the intellectual aspect of consciousness from unduly interfering with the expression of the total man. The practitioner of the *k'ai ho*, had, however, to be a sage first, and the technique was a recognized and respectable way of artistic production, closely connected to the basic ideas and the enlightenment of Taoism. It is thus defined by a leading Chinese artist:

> Where things grow and expand that is k'ai: where things are gathered up, that is ho. When you expand (k'ai) you should think of gathering up (ho) and then there will be structure; when you gather up (ho) then you should think of expanding (k'ai) and then you will have inexpressible effortlessness and an air of inexhaustible spirit. In using the brush, there is not a moment you can depart from the k'ai ho.[4]

A striking example of this is the "Branch of Plum Blossoms (see the plates in Chang Chung-yuan) by the artist who signed his name as Hsiao hsien Tzu (1459–1508). He was sent for by the court to paint a picture of pines and a running stream. As he was in front of the emperor he accidentally knocked over the jar of ink which splashed over the silk. "Taking advantage of the splashed ink, he made a wonderful drawing. The admiring emperor sighed and said: 'This is indeed the stroke of an immortal.' "[5]

Both surrealism and Taoism valued the unseen, intuitive aspect of man and developed a way of getting it to express itself. Surrealism, alchemy, and Oriental philosophies of unification involve a destruction or a reduction of the action of the ego or the consciousness conceived as the analytic intellect, and the affirmation of the validity of the darker, intuitive side of man.

What does all this have to do with Sartre? Is there a relationship between such opposites in Sartre, and if so what are the opposites? What was his attitude toward their unification and what would be the result of such a unification? The parallel terms in Sartre are the self and nonself, the consciousness and the external world, summed up by *pour-soi* and *en-soi*, although we should not attempt to translate Sartre's terms into precise terms of Chinese philosophy. But the fact is that the surrealists and the Chinese *approve* of this unification and of what it does to the consciousness, whereas Sartre would have disapproved of it, or simply asserted, as we have seen, that it was impossible, and rejected the effects it would have on the consciousness. He refused anything that would reduce the role or the potency of the subjectivity. Let us consider Sartre's discussion of the relation between these opposites.

In *L'Etre et le Néant*, Sartre described human reality as lack. That is, the *pour-soi* does not coincide with itself; it is not what it is. "Ce que le pour-soi manque, c'est le soi—ou soi-même comme en-soi."[6] The *pour-soi* therefore is failure, because it is the foundation only of its nothingness. *But* this failure does not make any sense to the *pour-soi* unless "il se saisit lui-même comme échec *en présence* de l'être qu'il a échoué à être, c'est-à-dire de l'être qui serait fondement de son être et non plus seulement fondement de son néant."[7]

Human reality is, therefore, a surpassing toward what it lacks, toward a coincidence with itself which is *never given*. Then Sartre invoked the rigor of the second Cartesian proof:

> . . . l'être imparfait se dépasse vers l'être parfait; l'être qui n'est fondement que de son néant se dépasse vers l'être qui est fondement de son être. Mais l'être vers quoi la réalité humaine se dépasse n'est pas un Dieu transcendant: il est au coeur d'elle-même, il n'est qu'elle-même comme totalité.[8]

This does not mean that the *pour-soi* transcends itself toward the *en-soi*, for if that were the case, it would coincide with "l'anéantissement de la conscience." This is basically what Sartre was accusing the surrealists of in *Littérature*. Consciousness then does not surpass itself toward its own annihilation, "elle ne veut pas se perdre dans l'en-soi d'identité à la limite de son dépassement. C'est pour le pour-soi en tant que tel que le pour-soi revendique l'être-en-soi."[9]

So the question arises, what then is this being toward which the *pour-soi* transcends itself, if it is not the *en-soi*? Sartre continued, "C'est l'impossible synthèse du pour-soi et de l'en-soi." Thus the *pour-soi* does not surpass itself toward the *en-soi*, where consciousness would be annihilated, rather it transcends itself toward the synthesis of the *en-soi* and the *pour-soi*, which allows it to retain the "translucidité nécessaire de la conscience en même temps que la coincidence avec soi de l'être-en-soi."[10]

But then Sartre just said that this totality, this synthesis, was impossible. That is why the being of human reality is suffering, "parce qu'elle surgit à l'être comme perpétuellement hantée par une totalité qu'elle est sans pouvoir l'être, puisque justement *elle ne pourrait atteindre l'en-soi sans se perdre comme pour-soi*.[11] [My emphasis] What then is the status of this totality? Can we say that it does not exist? At this point in the development of his thought, Sartre refused to say that it does not exist. He preferred rather to say that it cannot be realized.

Earlier Sartre attempted to clarify this idea by the image of the crescent moon: there are three parts to a crescent moon—the crescent, the dark part (i.e., that which is missing to the crescent), and the total moon. Now the crescent moon cannot exist by itself because the idea of crescent depends for its meaning on the totality, the full moon. The crescent cannot surpass itself toward the dark part, the missing part, for then it would no longer have that which is necessary for the definition of a crescent (the *pour-soi* cannot surpass itself toward the *en-soi* without the annihilation of consciousness). The crescent makes sense only by surpassing itself toward the synthesis of the crescent and the dark part, which is the synthesis of the two, or the totality. It then makes sense as a crescent and remains a crescent. Sartre did not say that this totality, this full moon, did not exist, only that a crescent moon cannot be a full moon. But we should not lose sight of another basic character of this Sartrean duality, and that is, ironically, its unity. For in this unity also lies the idea of facticity, since the *pour-soi* is rooted in the *en-soi*: "On sait qu'il n'y a point, d'une part, un pour-soi et, d'autre part, un monde, comme deux touts fermés dont il faudrait ensuite chercher comment ils communiquent. Mais le pour-soi est par lui-même rapport au monde. . . ."[12]

We are being-in-the-world, and yet not one with the world. Therefore it appears that we know suffering because we cannot become one with the totality of being but, if we did, we would lose the *pour-soi*. This is really a quandary. We exist with a duality whose unification haunts us, but which, if we achieved it would destroy consciousness, the *pour-soi*! It is not surprising then that the *pour-soi* cannot be indifferent to the *en-soi*, that man cannot help but react to objects in the external world: *La Nausée* is, in a large part, the story of the impact of that external world on man's consciousness. Furthermore, if this relation of self and world which Sartre made is descriptive and not prescriptive, it would also explain why the surrealists were preoccupied, almost hypnotized, by the object. As we shall see, however, this relation is probably more prescriptive, that is, moral, than otherwise.

It is a little hard to understand that in *L'Etre et le Néant*, Sartre in effect admitted the existence of this unity although he rejected its realization. The surrealist and the Taoist would also admit its existence but would believe in the possibility of its realization, and indeed highly recommend it, for therein lies the unification of human reality and even the destruction of that suffering which Sartre said is the result of this impossibility of unification. We should point out that Buddhism was developed as the solution to suffering.

Thus there is a Sartrean duality, parallel to the surrealist and Oriental dualities, but whereas the latter devote their efforts to unifying the two, Sartre made it his goal to keep them distinct. He achieved this separation basically by the ontological categories of the *pour-soi* and the *en-soi*, the first of which depends for its very existence on being separate from the latter, while at the same time being rooted in it. He rejected the surrealist world where objectivity and subjectivity are destroyed, where the discreteness and identity of the object in the external world are severely weakened, even destroyed; where lucidity is not valued, or is at least redefined; where abnormal states of mind, even madness are accepted; where consciousness, hence the cogito, loses its importance.

As long as we value consciousness and reject the trap of the subconscious, as long as we use language as a tool to keep the external world in control, so long will we retain that Sartrean lucidity and avoid what we will frequently refer to as the surrealist world. In *L'Etre et le Néant*, Sartre defined his categories and consequently brought the external world under control. We never see it break out again in his work as it did in *La Nausée* (where Roquentin confronts the object in nausea, the taste of facticity) under the pressure of the swarming, omnipresent *en-soi*. By 1946, as we have seen in *Littérature*, Sartre was ready to put the *objet surréaliste* in its place.

What are the characteristics of that surrealist world then, and where and for what reasons did it show up in Sartre's work? These are the questions to be answered in the following sections.

The Character of the Surrealist World

The vision of the surrealist world is presented under two aspects—the linguistic and the visual, both of which have the common characteristic that they are used to confront images and concepts which are not found to be so associated in the real world. It is doubtful if the surrealists ever actually had a perception of something that does not exist at all in the real world; most of their images are distortions of recognizable objects, or arbitrary associations of words or objects that do not exist in that relationship in common-sense perception. It is even doubtful, in any case, whether any man can imagine something that is purely fictitious in the most extreme sense of the word pure. A simplistic example is that of the winged horse: both parts of the image are found in the real world, i.e., the wings and the horse. The imaginative part lies in the association of the two aspects. It is possible to paint things which are not recognizable, but in that case we get very near to nonrepresentational art, and it is questionable whether we can even talk of such a thing as presenting an image of the external world.

In the realm of language, even the surrealists had to work with existing words, and creation lay in associating them. It is true that the dadaists invented words, but the nonsense poetry that came out of such an effort holds very little lasting interest for poetry or surrealist activity. The purest activity of automatic writing obviously comes out to be in the French language, or the English language, etc. The actual invention by the surrealists of linguistic or visual images was based to some extent on the common-sense world of everyday perception. The linguistic and visual aspects of the surrealist world are similar in the quality of their impact: it is almost invariably disturbing, as we shall see.

On the linguistic level, surrealist poetry attacks syntax and dismantles the sentence; however, there is more talk of this approach than actual practice, for many surrealist "poems" are not unreadable from the point of view of structure, but merely incoherent from the point of view of imagery and meaning. As we have just suggested, dismantling the language has to stop at the level of the word or the result is gibberish.

From the Sartrean point of view, the surrealists are using the language as poets do—they refuse to use it as a tool. This corresponds to their attitude toward the object, which, as the *objet surréaliste*, was nonutilitarian. Prose, for Sartre, allows man to communicate effectively, etc., thereby directly allowing the writer to be committed, for language is no longer the end product as is the case with the poet. As we have remarked in Part I, the surrealists "use" language, but not in any way acceptable for Sartre, for their use is as a tool in surrealist activity. Breton attacked realism and the novel in the *Premier manifeste* as a debasement of language, reducing literature, in effect, to a pastime; "Si le style d'information pure et simple . . . a cours presque seul dans les romans, c'est, il faut le reconnaître, que l'ambition des auteurs ne va pas très loin."[13] Language then is not for the transfer of information, and authors who believe that that is its function, simply are unaware of its possibilities for surrealist research.

If we have dismantled language down to the word, that beyond which we cannot go without a total breakdown, it follows that surrealist effort may most easily be focused on the image as association of words. Breton felt unprepared to categorize the types of images, but he points out their common virtue in the *Premier manifeste*:

> Pour moi, la plus forte est celle qui présente le degré d'arbitraire le plus élevé, . . . celle qu'on met le plus longtemps à traduire en langage pratique, soit qu'elle recèle une dose énorme de contradiction apparente, soit que l'un de ses termes en soit curieusement dérobé, . . . soit qu'elle tire d'elle-même une justification formelle dérisoire, soit qu'elle soit d'ordre hallucinatoire, soit qu'elle prête très naturellement à l'abstrait le masque du concret, ou inversement, soit qu'elle implique la négation de quelque propriété physique élémentaire, soit qu'elle déchaîne le rire.[14]

Nearly all the characteristics of the surrealist image in the above quotation apply just as well to painting and sculpture.

In the surrealist external world, objects lose their identity and their discreteness in accordance with the stated ideal of perceiving things from the point of noncontradiction—reducing the external world, in effect, to a state of nondifferentiation. Obviously they were not totally successful in achieving nondifferentiation, but the identity of objects weakened, and the principle of *critique-paranoïaque* made them interchangeable. This amounts to reducing the object to a Rorschach inkblot: one reality immediately suggests two or three more, so that any object may be treated in the same way. The result of this is that "Il est impossible d'accorder une valeur quelconque à la réalité (immédiate) puisque celle-ci peut en principe représenter, signifier n'importe quoi."[15] This technique is basically a development of the old dadaist readymade, closely related to the *objet surréaliste*, as we saw in Part I.

There are again two basic but sometimes interrelated reactions on the part of the surrealists toward this surrealist vision of things. In their own work we see the surrealist world as (1) *merveilleux*, marvelous, full of adventure; it seems to reflect the enthusiasm of explorers on a strange planet, wondering what will turn up next; and (2) frightening, with an oppressive feeling of a vague, tragic menace, of awful portents lurking behind apparently innocent appearances. This second characteristic is by far the more frequent. This is the world of a frightened child in a circus fun house, not quite sure but what it may be real. "L'esprit qui plonge dans le surréalisme revit avec exaltation la meilleure part de son enfance,"[16] writes Breton in the *Premier manifeste*.

> On revit, dans l'ombre, une *terreur précieuse* . . . On traverse, avec un tressaillement, ce que les occultistes appellent des paysages dangereux. Je suscite sur mes pas des monstres qui guettent; ils ne sont pas encore trop malintentionnés à mon égard et je ne suis pas perdu, puisque je les crains. Voici "les éléphants à tête de femme et les lions volants" que Soupault et moi nous tremblâmes naguère de rencontrer.[17] [My emphasis]

This menace is obvious to anyone who thumbs through a history of surrealist painting. It is found in the early Chirico, in Max Ernst's "Monument aux oiseaux," "La Nuit d'amour," and in "Deux Enfants sont menacés par un rossignol," to mention only three of his works. In the last, a nightingale, usually associated with song and romance, appears to harbor some hidden dread. One child is lying on the ground, the father flees with another in his arms, while the mother has a club fending off the bird. Picabia, Miro, Tanguy, and Magritte (Le Viol, Le Mouvement perpétuel, L'Ange migrateur, La Condition humaine, Le Dormeur téméraire, etc.) give the same feeling. Man Ray's photograph "Primat de la matière sur la pensée"[18] gives a striking example of an object from the real world becoming viscous, losing little by little its identity, becoming unstable and flowing out of its borders. This is a photograph of a nude, lying on her back with one knee slightly bent, anatomically explicit. But where she comes into contact with whatever she is lying on, her flesh has flowed like warm wax, broken out of the usually attractive and erotic contour of thigh, hip, and waist.

I would hesitate to insist too much on the title of this photograph, but "primacy of matter over thought" demonstrates precisely what we have been suggesting all through this study and will show up in *La Nausée*: namely, that matter (or undifferentiated nature, that with which man has no technological relationship) is there, lying in wait as it were, scarcely held in control and in coherent form by the intellect. That Man Ray should choose an object such as a nude, an attractive, preoccupying object, to portray this concept, emphasizes the disturbing effect on the perceiver. This is the formless, threatening world that the surrealist tries to get hold of by automatism, by restraining the intellect, the world that he actively desires to see although it may be frightening. It is the same world that intrudes on Roquentin, against his will. In a Sartrean sense, this photograph could well be called "Facticity," or man's necessary connection with the *en-soi*. It seems to sum up the whole problem of duality—all that is left is to take a moral attitude toward it.

This viscous menace shows up most in Salvador Dali (there is not much point in listing all the minor surrealist painters and their works, nor in belaboring the point) in such things as "Le Jeu lugubre," "l'Accommodation des désirs," "Naissance des désirs liquides," "La Persistance de la mémoire," "Méditation sur la harpe,"—the titles alone suggest this content. Dali is a good craftsman: we can usually recognize the elements of his paintings from our common-sense perception of the everyday world. These pieces are photographic in their detail, but are nightmarish in the ensemble—much as Breton used everyday words to create a terrifying image. In some cases they are parts of the common-place world of objects or persons which have "run," flowed out of their borders, producing large amorphous lumps or protuberances supported by crutches. It is the claim of this study that this amorphous, viscous, threatening world of Dali and the surrealists in general, is the same world that intruded on Roquentin that day in the park.

The question now is, if the surrealists sought a vision of the inter-identity of objects, a vision of nondifferentiation, a vision of Nature, a vision of that point where things are no longer perceived as contradictory, then why does this image or the effort to see this image result in a feeling of menace? Why is terror such a part of the surrealist world, if indeed the surrealists were so eager to have that vision of things? Why does automatism, if indeed we assume that such a technique is operative, why does automatism produce such a vision of the external world in the name of *critique-paranoïaque*, *hasard objectif*, and the point of noncontradiction, whereas a roughly similar technique, the *k'ai ho*, never produces such a thing? On the contrary (see the plates in *Taoism and Creativity*, by Chang Chung-yuan) the *k'ai ho*, practiced by the artist-sage who has the Tao, who understands nondifferentiation, produces works reflecting the yin and yang—that quiescence and movement which are the origins of all creativity—and his work of art in its own harmony is a mirror of that cosmic harmony intuited by the artist. I suggest it is because the surrealist in not an artist-sage, he is a kind of researcher seeking a glimpse of what the Taoist artist-sage already knew. The immediate answer to all these questions is that the surrealist, in spite of his lip service and even real concern for the idea of noncontradiction, is still an Occidental, infected beyond cure with the utilitarian attitude toward the external world—an attitude deeply ingrained in him from the platonic, Christian, Cartesian duality that set the external world apart from the self as a thing foreign, therefore threatening, therefore to be controlled, and manipulated by technology. The menacing aspect of surrealist poetry and painting is the measure of its failure to find the point of noncontradiction.

That the surrealist is an Occidental in spite of himself is only a surface explanation obviously, and does not really explain why the art of the Orient is different from Western art. That difference could be explained only by a profound knowledge of Eastern and Western attitudes, and in cultural or biological surmises going back perhaps to prehistory: "Philosophical speculation in China may well have grown out of the very ancient naturalistic conceptions of the alternating seasons," writes Grousset, "Its origins go back to the speculations of prehistoric diviners. . . ."[19]

At any rate, the surrealist vision of the external world is menacing for the same reason that Roquentin finds it menacing. When we assert then that Roquentin's vision is surrealistic, it certainly does not mean that it is Oriental. Even as Sartre disapproved of the nonutilitarian object and sees in Nature that nontechnological relationship of man to things, a viscous and threatening presence, so also does the surrealist have the same attitude toward such nonutilitarian things in spite of the fact that he provokes the image of that world and finds it marvelous but threatening. For the surrealist it is necessary to provoke that image, but that image intrudes painfully on Roquentin.

As we have suggested before, the vision of this unstable world of objects is apparently not impossible to achieve, but, as in the case of Sartre, achieving it may be condemned on grounds of lucidity, freedom, etc. The point is that one ought not to achieve it, particularly not as a permanent condition, and when we go from what is to what ought to be, we have made a moral decision. And this point bears emphasis: the surrealist seeks the vision, even though it is threatening; sometimes, the aspect of the *merveilleux* even outweighs the menace, but not frequently. The surrealists, after all, were disoriented by relativity, by the breakdown of rationalism, by the distrust of a technology which keeps at bay the monsters of the West. Nontechnological man cannot control his environment and therefore, as in *Beowulf*, as in many primitive mythologies, sees monsters in the external world and in the forces of nature. It is no accident that that aspect of Romanticism which loves and praises nature coincides with the industrial revolution. Because not only does man miss the trees and mountains in the industrialized city, but he can afford to love them because they are no longer out of his control. This assertion would allow us to see why the industrial revolution began in England, developed later in Germany, and even later in France—paralleling the development of Romanticism.

Nature is a monster for Sartre too, but he will keep it at bay by the lucidity and the preservation of the *pour-soi*. Even at this early stage Sartre sees man as technological par excellence, which is, of course, also a tendency of Marxism toward which he was to gravitate more and more. Thus, as we remarked in Part I, the surrealist is in a real sense anti-Marxist. Now that we have given a larger picture of the meaning of unification, described the surrealist vision of the external world, and surmised on its varying impact let us see how the external world fares in Sartre's *La Nausée*.

La Nausée

This is the story of a metaphysical reaction to the human condition, not a practical socio-politico-economic appraisal of the situation of the proletariat. From the Communist point of view then, as we pointed out previously, the early Sartre shared a common approach with the surrealists: It is one that he apparently outgrew, but which was always of prime concern to the surrealists.

Sartre accused the surrealists in *Littérature* of inaction: their perception of the point of noncontradiction, a perception made in relation to the object, would obviate action and therefore would be inimical to the revolution of the proletariat. The grim surrealist vision of the external world is therefore parallel in a sense to Roquentin's nausea. Kern remarks that both the terms "absurdity" and "nausea" were used by Nietzsche and Sartre "and that both thinkers see man's experiencing them as resulting in inaction."[20] Both surrealism and Sartrean nausea then are metaphysical attitudes promoting inaction. Roquentin is not a revolutionary.

Nausea, the taste of facticity, the actual physical sensation (the somatic knowledge, so to speak) of man's connection to the *en-soi*, is the knowledge of one's existence as different from the external world, and at the same time as one with it. That is to say, Roquentin experiences his existence in nausea, but that experience is not a result of intellectual processes, of imagination, etc., but comes about *only* by a confrontation with the object. One must come face-to-face with the bare, nontechnological, nonhumanized, nonutilitarian object to experience nausea. Thus nausea is again seen as nearly parallel to that surrealist point of noncontradiction, but is a reaction of dread with none of the surrealist enthusiasm.

Nausea is a particularly appropriate term (in spite of the fact that *Melancholia* was the original title to the novel) because it emphasizes the physical, nonintellectual aspect of the experience. When Roquentin finds language no longer effective in keeping this world of Nature at bay, i.e., when the intellectual defenses temporarily fail him, that world of unstable objects intrudes and he experiences nausea. This is the condition the surrealists sought, when reason was suppressed and that formless world was allowed to appear. Roquentin has fulfilled the criteria for automatism in his vision of the bus seat that could become a dead donkey and in his experiences in the park, perceiving the world in terms of the *critique-paranoïaque*. But he did not want to. Was he forced to, condemned to?

Roquentin is the type of Western, technological man: he has come up against that formless world and he does not like it. He experienced nausea for the same reason that the bulk of surrealist painting shows a menacing world of objects—Western man has a deeply ingrained distrust of unification and nondifferentiation. But Roquentin is no common Occidental, at least he does not stop with fear and rejection. He has had nausea, known the point of noncontradiction for awhile in the garden, but refuses to remain in it. He says that he may never be rid of the nausea, but he returns to a life of lucidity. This is parallel to the Buddhist who knows Nirvana but returns to the world, as will become plainer as we go on.

Roquentin's description of his experiences in the park, and his consequent use of the word absurdity ("Le mot absurdité naît à présent sous ma plume.")[21] is a verbalization *after* the experience. The experience of *nausée*, or as we have suggested, of nondifferentiation, was ineffable, just as all the Oriental philosophies of unification describe their enlightenment. We should recall at this point the Taoist parallel of the net that catches the fish mentioned in Part I: not only is it impossible to have the enlightenment as a result of verbal description and explanation, but that very conceptualization prevents the experience from coming about. So Roquentin, looking back on his experience in the park, says that the word absurdity was born under his pen; but

> tout à l'heure, au jardin, je ne l'ai pas trouvé, mais je ne le cherchais pas non plus, je n'en avais pas besoin: je pensais sans mots, *sur* les choses, avec les choses. L'absurdité, ce n'était pas une idée dans ma tête, ni un souffle de voix. . . . Et sans rien formuler nettement, je comprenais que j'avais trouvé la clé de l'Existence. . . . Absurdité: encore un mot; je me débats contre des mots; là-bas, je touchais la chose. . . . Oh! comment pourrai-je fixer ça avec des mots? (182–183)

It is as the Taoist says: the Tao which is called the Tao is not the Tao.

I am not going to quote at great length from this section, but only enough to give an impression of what is happening. We can get some idea from this scene of the importance of language to Sartre, particularly discursive prose, because in its absence we may perceive nondifferentiation; the use of language is of immense importance to a culture that treats the external world in a utilitarian way. This part of *La Nausée* is the most amazing description I have read outside of Chinese philosophy of the experience of nondifferentiation, and perhaps the only one in my experience with Western literature (if we except such popularizations as those of D. T. Suzuki and Alan Watts during the 1950s). The experience of Nirvana (for example) and Sartrean nausea are similar: both are nonverbal and ineffable; one may return from them to "ordinary" life, but one is never quite the same after. Even descriptions of those Eastern "enlightenments" are not done with quite the same lucidity as here: they are usually explained in aphorisms, with actions, in imagery, or seemingly irrelevant or contradictory statements. And Sartre has done this in prose.

This is the place to point out that we cannot qualify nausea as "bad," but rather as a valuable if painful experience of the whole man. "La nausée ne m'a pas quitté et je ne crois pas qu'elle me quittera . . . mais . . . ce n'est plus une maladie ni une quinte passagère: c'est moi." (179)

Let us survey the role of objects in *La Nausée*, compare them with a probable surrealist reaction to them, and consider the reasons for the various reactions. Roquentin realizes from the very beginning that his problem is somehow bound up with his perception of objects. It is not clear why the formless world of Nature began to intrude little by little on Roquentin, unless he had become disenchanted with the work of the intellect, particularly as history, seeing that his book on the marquis de Rollebon was leading him nowhere. Still, he made no effort to reject reason as the surrealists did as a result of their own disenchantment. He was ripe to become a surrealist, he was emotionally in the same condition the budding surrealists were in 1919, but he held on all the more tightly to his lucidity and rejected that Nature. His effort to understand his problem is analytical, not intuitive. In a real sense then, *La Nausée* was Sartre's admission that that unstable world exists, but also his definitive rejection of it.

Why did Roquentin find that surreal world menacing and why did he reject it? Why is it that he "longs for a world which is truly and authentically named?"[22] Which would therefore allow him to take "possession of the world both physically and intellectually"?[23] Because he accepts the Western dualism which demands a technological relation to objects, and makes language a tool in that technology. Thus Sartre, even in his option for prose, that useful language, was an Occidental and a moralist on his way to Marxism. He accused the surrealists in *Littérature* of using literature to destroy language. This is saying, in effect, that the surrealist poet misuses language to break down man's technological relationship with the world (intentionally doing what inadvertently happened to Roquentin in the bus, when the seat lost its form). Such a "misuse" of language and its effect on the world of objects implies a relation between the word and the referent which is practically magical. But it is no more magical, after all, than Sartre's ideal use of language as a tool with an "almost mystical power to conjure up realities that previously did not exist even as potentialities."[24] Naming "seemed to him capable not only of revealing but even of changing reality."[25] The surrealists too had concluded that they could impose their desire on the world through language, and went at the task with enthusiasm. Such contrary views about the use of language, however, do not hide a common belief about the nature of language; namely, that it is closely connected to the world of things, and can be used to affect that world. As we have often remarked, the decision on the use of language remains a moral one.

Roquentin's first experience is with the well-known and often-described muddy pebble, a disturbing contact with the *en-soi*. Jean Arp also picked up pebbles from the beaches, but he sketched them, worked over them, attempting to simplify their chance forms and catch their essence in "ovales mouvants, symboles de la métamorphose et du devenir des corps."[26] In some of his *bois gravés* he took advantage of the grain of the wood, "où s'inscrivaient l'histoire de l'arbre lui-même et les vicissitudes des saisons. . . ."[27] In such a way his own subjectivity came into contact with the chance forms of nature to produce an artifact, a piece of art. His technique was basically that of a surrealist "Rorschach" image to force inspiration. It too was a contact with an *en-soi*, but with the intention of touching nature, a reaction quite different from Roquentin's, and an example of a surrealist provocation of that experience. On the other hand, perhaps Arp was deceiving himself, and performing an esthetic *analyse bourgeoise* on the rocks, never really coming in contact with Nature.

The part of *La Nausée* which particularly concerns us is that of Roquentin's awakening to the realization of that formless Nature that we have called the surrealist world and to the reaction necessary to that perception. For Roquentin it seems to be a starting point; for the surrealists that vision comes near to being the goal.

Objects are acutely present in *La Nausée*, to such a point that Sartre's accusation that the surrealists were materialists because they practiced their destructions on objects and were so preoccupied with objects, applies as well to the Sartre of *La Nausée*. There are innumerable smaller and less extreme confrontations with objects than the one in the park, but we will confine ourselves for the most part to the great crises, particularly to things building up to those crises. We should note, too, that Roquentin feels more comfortable with mineral objects than with organic ones: this has been frequently pointed out by critics. It is true that these mineral objects do not have a life of their own ["Les pierres, c'est dur et ça ne bouge pas." (41)], but they are still basically the external world, the *en-soi*, and in metaphysical terms are just as foreign to man as plants, in fact, more so, since they are inorganic. Roquentin is probably reflecting Sartre's own personal discomfort before nature as we saw in Part I. He remarks that Bouville is besieged by vegetation on only three sides, "Sur le quatrième côté, il y a un grand trou, plein d'une eau noire qui remue toute seule." (220) We have previously seen that both Sartre (according to Simone de Beauvoir) and Baudelaire (according to Sartre) could tolerate the sea, which was accepted as a kind of mineral.

Before Roquentin really understands what is going on, he has a kind of intuition of things to come, a predisposition so to speak, for the kind of experience he will have: he has what amounts to a surrealist fascination with pieces of junk and trash he picks up in the street: "J'aime beaucoup ramasser les marrons, les vieilles loques, surtout les papiers. Il m'est agréable de les prendre, de fermer ma main sur eux; pour un peu je les porterais à ma bouche comme font les enfants." (21) He inspects the different kinds of leaves, some crisp and new, "palpitants . . . posés comme des cygnes . . . ," others smashed, withered, and mashed into the mud: "Tout cela est bon à prendre. Quelquefois je les palpe simplement en les regardant de tout près. . . ." (21) He sees an officer with tan boots step over a piece of paper lying beside a puddle, and goes to pick it up.

> C'était une page réglée, arrachée sans doute à un cahier d'école. La pluie l'avait trempée et tordue, elle était couverte de cloques et de boursouflures, comme une main brûlée. Le trait rouge de la marge avait déteint en une buée rose; l'encre avait coulé par endroits. Le bas de la page disparaissait sous une croûte de boue. Je me suis baissé, je me réjouissais déjà de toucher cette pâte tendre et fraîche qui se roulerait sous mes doigts en boulettes grises . . . Je n'ai pas pu.
>
> Je suis resté courbé, une seconde, j'ai lu "Dictée: le Hibou blanc. . . . (22)

All he has to do is pick this up and put it in a frame and he has an *objet surréaliste*, cryptic, banal phrase and all. Marcel Duchamp exhibited similar pieces of torn ruled paper on the case of his "La mariée mise à nu par ses célibataires, même," arranged in an apparently haphazard way, and bearing such phrases as "La Pendule de profil, et l'Inspecteur d'espace."[28] Torn paper was a common ingredient of surrealist collages.

But he cannot pick it up because if he did he would be putting himself into a nonutilitarian relationship with it, and would then lose his privileged position in what amounts to a dual, utilitarian world of *l'analyse bourgeoise*, again perfiguring Sartre's later gravitation toward Marxism. As we see, Roquentin is no surrealist because

> Les objets, cela ne devrait pas toucher, puisque cela ne vit pas. On s'en sert, on les remet en place, on vit au milieu d'eux; ils sont utiles, rien de plus. Et moi, ils me touchent, c'est insupportable. J'ai peur d'entrer en contact avec eux. . . . (22)

And so Roquentin successfully fends off nausea for the time being, the image of things in their raw thingness. Not only are objects in the external world the focus of his curiosity, his body also comes under the same scrutiny. The scene with the mirror (30–31) can be seen as a preparation for the self-inflicted wound (141–143), and for that reason we will consider them at the same time.

Roquentin is on the point of treating his body as if it were another thing in the external world. Such an attitude is not uncommon among the proponents of the judaeo-christian-platonic ethic. If one's identity is bound up with the immortal soul, one gets a great deal of comfort from knowing that he is not his body which is so obviously mortal: even the linguistic habit of referring to one's body as "it" emphasizes the duality. "All flesh is grass," wrote the prophet (Isaiah 40:6), but the soul-body duality frees one from mortality. "Au fond, je suis même choqué qu'on puisse lui attribuer des qualités de ce genre, comme si on appelait beau ou laid un morceau de terre ou bien un bloc de rocher," writes Roquentin of his body. (30) He contemplates his face up close in the mirror; the nose and the mouth, everything human disappears:

> Des rides brunes de chaque côté du gonflement fiévreux des lèvres, des crevasses, des taupinières. Un soyeux duvet blanc court sur les grandes pentes des joues, deux poils sortent des narines: c'est une carte géologique en relief. Et, malgré tout, ce monde lunaire m'est familier. Je ne peux pas dire que j'en *reconnaisse* les détails. Mais l'ensemble me fait une impression de déjà vu qui m'engourdit: je glisse doucement dans le sommeil. (31)

Here is a thing which is *his* only in a vague way. Although I would not want to insist on it, this vision of one's face as something not intimately connected with one's identity, a face eroded and crevassed like a relief map, and the very interest with which one contemplates it in the mirror suggests, from my own experience with the drug, the type of preoccupation and the character of the perception provoked by the use of mescaline. In 1935, three years before the publication of *La Nausée*, Sartre had taken an injection of mescaline which resulted in about six months of depression and hallucinations: "Il avait vu des parapluies-vautours, des souliers-squelettes, de monstrueux visages; et, sur ses côtés, par derrière, grouillaient des crabes, des poulpes, des choses grimaçants."[29]

Immediately after the paragraph quoted above, Roquentin writes, "Je voudrais me ressaisir: une sensation vive et tranchée me délivrerait." (31) Why does he want to regrasp himself? Not simply because he is getting sleepy and wants to wake up, but because his body is slipping away from him into the world of the *en-soi*, into that extreme world of dualism where the body is no longer the self. And what is this "sensation vive et tranchée" that would deliver him? It is the stab in the hand that he was to give himself later. (142) But he does not stab himself this time:

> Je plaque ma main gauche contre ma joue, je tire sur la peau; je me fais la grimace. Toute une moitié de mon visage cède, la moitié gauche de la bouche se tord et s'enfle, en découvrant une dent, l'orbite s'ouvre sur un globe blanc, sur une chair rose et saignante. Ce n'est pas ce que je cherchais: rien de fort, rien de neuf; du doux, du flou, du déjà vu. (31)

And so he is unsuccessful, his efforts produce nothing new—just a view of some flabby skin and a bloodshot eye. But he is more successful in his next confrontation with his body. This time it is a question of his hand which takes on life of its own, becomes a thing. Sitting at his desk, he looks at it:

> Elle est sur le dos. Elle me montre son ventre gras. Elle a l'air d'une bête à la renverse. Les doigts, ce sont les pattes. Je m'amuse à les faire remuer, très vite, comme les pattes d'un crabe qui est tombé sur le dos. (141)

This hand is obviously his, even he, but that apparent fact seems to grow doubtful: "C'est moi, ces deux bêtes qui s'agitent au bout de mes bras. Ma main gratte une de ses pattes, avec l'ongle d'une autre patte. . . ." (141) As he continues thinking along this line, the duality grows stronger: his identity is associated with his thought, but his body goes about its business.

> . . . cette espèce de rumination douloureuse: *j'existe*, c'est moi qui l'entretiens. Moi. Le corps, ça vit tout seul, une fois que ça a commencé. Mais la pensée, c'est moi qui la continue, qui la déroule. . . . Ma pensée, c'est *moi*: voilà pourquoi je ne peux pas m'arrêter. J'existe parce que je pense . . . et je ne peux pas m'empêcher de penser. (142)

These thoughts on Cartesian dualism, the *cogito* as proof of existence of thought but not of body, build up to a frenzy:

> Les pensées naissent par-derrière moi comme un vertige, je les sens naître derrière ma tête . . . si je cède, elles vont venir là devant, entre mes yeux—et si je cède toujours, la pensée grossit, grossit et la voilà, immense, qui me remplit tout entier et renouvelle mon existence. (143)

He opens his knife and gives himself "un bon coup de couteau dans la paume." (143) And it bleeds:

> Et puis après? qu'est'ce qu'il y a de changé? Tout de même, je regarde avec satisfaction, sur la feuille blanche, en travers des lignes que j'ai tracées tout à l'heure, cette petite mare de sang qui a cessé enfin d'être moi. (143)

There is some satisfaction here at least; there was none before the mirror. This "sensation vive et tranchée" is more effective. If this little pool of blood has finally ceased being he, by implication the rest of his body *is* he. Whereas in both the scenes just discussed he has described his body as having the same alien, vaguely menacing aspect that he has described in objects in the "Surrealist" world.

Douglas explains that the knife-thrust is going to nihilize (he is undoubtedly translating "néantir," which Hazel Barnes translates as "nihilate"), that the stab is going to nihilize Roquentin's body.[30] But if that is the case, the result of that act would be that Roquentin's body is differentiated from Roquentin, putting a distance between it and him, turning the body into a thing. Thus the dualism is reinforced. I believe that Roquentin is "redeeming his body . . . giving it to himself," as Douglas puts it, but in another sense: He is recalling to himself, to his own identity, a body that was just about to stray away from him into the *en-soi*, into the world of things, into the menacing surrealist world, where faces are mountains and valleys, and hands are animals. The frantic stab into his hand was an effort, a healthy effort on the part of an Occidental just about to carry his mind-body dualism (his concern for the purity of the *pour-soi*) too far. He has, in effect, succeeded in regrasping himself ("ressaisir" was the word he used before the mirror). Douglas seems to think that Roquentin is *trying* to turn his body into an *en-soi* in order to be his own foundation, and to possess his body in an act with sexual overtones (the stabbing, etc.) as if it were the Other. "Man's basic self-contradictory aim . . . is to be his own foundation, *ens causa sui*, to reach the satisfying fullness and self-identity of the object, while yet remaining sufficiently distinguished from this self to be conscious of it."[31] If, as Douglas states, Roquentin stabbed his hand in order to get in touch with the *en-soi* (to appropriate the *en-soi* for himself, thereby gaining being while retaining the *pour-soi*, or nonbeing), then we have to assume that he was acting as a surrealist—since his act would have the aim of destroying or at least weakening the opposites, getting his *pour-soi* and *en-soi* together and becoming God, intentionally provoking the intuition. But Roquentin has never given any other indication in this book that he was the kind of person to do such a thing, to provoke contact with the *en-soi*, to weaken the *pour-soi*. And why should Roquentin wish to get into possession of something that is admittedly menacing, which he perceives as alien? The *en-soi* has been acting pretty strangely lately for that sort of thing.

If, as I feel, Roquentin is an Occidental who does not give in to a desire for unification of opposites, for appropriating being as his own and becoming God, then his self-inflicted wound is not a surrealist effort, but rather the healthy act of a man who sees the dangers of total duality: if he does not seek unification, neither does he go overboard and accept the extreme consequences of Cartesian dualism. Jung remarked that the Chinese always recognized the paradoxes, the polarity basic to what is alive: "The opposites always balanced one another—a sign of high culture. One-sidedness, though it lends momentum, is a mark of barbarism."[32] We must come from reading *La Nausée* with the conviction that Roquentin is a well-balanced man, a stable individual who is willing to take seriously anything that has merit, but who will not go to extremes in any direction. He is, after all, in a very real sense Sartre, as Sartre admitted in *Les Mots*. We have already discussed this point in connection with the parallel between nausea and the point of noncontradiction.

If Roquentin stabbed his hand because of his "unattainable longing to become God"[33] (in Sartrean terms, to be *en-soi* and *pour-soi* at the same time, being and nonbeing), then it seems we must conclude that he committed a surrealist act, that he was provoking an intuition of unification. I prefer to see Roquentin as a dreamer who pinches himself to bring himself back to the real world. A surrealist does not destroy a dream and Roquentin did not want his body to become the Other. The Sartrean man does not provoke such experiences, he undergoes them, as we shall soon see. We have just remarked that Roquentin saw his body becoming, in effect, the Other. Sartre pointed out that this is the very problem in the relation between consciousness and body: "mais ces difficultés proviennent de ce que je tente d'unir ma conscience non à *mon* corps mais au corps *des autres*."[34] And thus we maintain in this study that Roquentin was trying to retrieve his body from otherness, not drive it into otherness (which is the effect of nihilation), to make it part of himself, to make it himself as part of his identity, for man is in real danger of perceiving himself from the point of view of the Other (as we see in "Enfance d'un chef," *Huis clos, Le Diable et le bon Dieu*, etc.):

> Car ma main me révèle la résistance des objets, leur dureté ou leur mollesse et non *elle-même*. Ainsi ne vois-je pas ma main autrement que je ne vois cet encrier. Je déploie une distance de moi à elle et cette distance vient s'intégrer dans les distances que j'établis entre tous les objets du monde.[35]

The next major crisis comes in the bus after Roquentin has ended his evening with the self-taught man. We have previously remarked on the value of language in controlling the formless, unstable world of Nature, and here we see it breaking down and allowing a surrealist *critique-par-anoïaque* to operate. In spite of his efforts to control this instability by the magic of language ("Je murmure: c'est une banquette, un peu comme un exorcisme''), things lose their names (''les choses sont délivrées de leurs noms,'') and the bus seat flows out of its borders:

> Elle reste ce qu'elle est, avec sa peluche rouge, milliers de petites pattes rouges, en l'air, toutes raides, de petites pattes mortes. Cet énorme ventre tourne en l'air sanglant, ballonné—boursouflé avec toutes ses pattes mortes, ventre qui flotte dans cette boîte, dans ce ciel gris, ce n'est pas une banquette. (177)

This surrealist vision of things is not provoked, just as a vision of unification or the appropriation of the *en-soi* was not provoked by the handstabbing affair. Kern summarizes the whole Sartrean-surrealist relationship in a nutshell: ''Had Roquentin been created by Sartre in the image of a surrealist poet, he would have reveled in the newness of his experience and poetically rendered the unwonted world he perceived while riding on the streetcar.''[36] And if he had been a painter, he would have painted it; it would have been a horrible, menacing picture, even for him, but he would have done it. But what about Sartre? He turned this experience into literature—does that make him a surrealist? If Sartre was indeed Roquentin, has he not reproduced the experience he had in the bus? A partial answer to this rather rhetorical question might be that he did not give it to us in a poem or a painting, but in very Sartrean fashion: in lucid, analytic prose. This and the scene in the park, which follows it, may be, in fact, two of the very few *prose* descriptions of the experience of the surrealist world—they are usually in poetry, or by visual means.

The often-described tree and its roots in the park are like a painting by Salvador Dali, and as we have seen, that is no accident. We would emphasize that these visions were not provoked by Roquentin; all those objects bothered him, and forced themselves on him:

> Ils m'incommodaient; j'aurais souhaité qu'ils existassent moins fort, d'une façon plus sèche, plus abstraite, avec plus de retenu. Le marronnier se pressait contre mes yeux. (181)

The last vision of that unstable world of Nature, which Roquentin describes upon his return from Paris, has likewise the same menacing surrealist character, the same changing identities, the same lack of integrity on the part of the object. A man out walking may see a rag blowing down the street,

> et quand le chiffon sera tout près de lui, il verra que c'est un quartier de viande pourrie, maculé de poussière, qui se traine en rampant, en sautillant, un bout de chair torturée qui se roule dans les ruisseaux en projetant par spasmes des jets de sang. (224)

Extra eyes spring out on the cheeks of children, clothing comes alive, tongues become centipedes, sleepers awaken in foreign terrains, etc., etc., and all man's science and humanism, his "dignité de roseau pensant" (225) will be of little help. The *critique-paranoïaque* has taken over. Man is afraid in the midst of nature, writes Sartre, in *Baudelaire*, "c'est qu'il se sent pris dans une immense existence amorphe et gratuite . . . il n'a plus sa place nulle part, il est posé sur la terre, sans but, sans raison d'être, comme une bruyère ou une touffe de genêt."[37]

Our last problem is perhaps the most interesting and concerns the most enigmatic page in the book. As Roquentin sits in the park, stifled by existence, he makes an intellectual effort to regain his privileged position: "Je criai, 'Quelle saleté, Quelle Saleté!' et je me secouai pour me débarrasser de cette saleté poisseuse. . . ." (190) And almost immediately "le jardin se vida comme par un grand trou, le monde disparut de la même façon qu'il était venu . . . il restait de la terre jaune autour de moi, d'où sortait des branches mortes dressées en l'air." (190) He gets up and goes out.

Upon arriving at the gate, he turns around and looks back:

> Alors le jardin m'a souri. Je me suis appuyé à la grille et j'ai longtemps regardé. Le sourire des arbres, du massif de laurier, ça *voulait dire* quelque chose; c'était ça la véritable secret de l'existence. Je me rappelai qu'un dimanche, il n'y a pas plus de trois semaines, j'avais déjà saisi sur les choses une sorte d'air complice. Etait-ce à moi qu'il s'adressait? Je sentais avec ennui que je n'avais aucun moyen de comprendre. Aucun moyen. Pourtant c'était là, dans l'attente, ça ressemblait à un regard. C'était là, sur le tronc du marronnier . . . c'était *le* marronier. Les choses, on aurait dit des pensées qui s'arrêtaient en route, qui s'oubliaient, qui oubliaient ce qu'elles avaient voulu penser et qui restaient comme ça, ballottantes, avec un drôle de petit sens qui les dépassait. Ça m'agaçait ce petit sens: je ne pouvais pas le comprendre, quand bien même je serais resté cent ans appuyé à la grille; j'avais appris sur l'existence tout ce que je pouvais savoir. Je suis parti, je suis rentré à l'hôtel, et voilà, j'ai écrit. (191)

"Why did the garden smile at him?" that is the question. Champigny writes that "in opposition to crude existence," this scene "suggests a form of being which is more in accord with the Platonic vision. When Roquentin leaves the public park after his ecstasy, a different view of things is sketched. . . ."[38] The feeling that Roquentin then got from the park was not a "practical signal (things as tools), nor a religious sign . . .; it is an esthetic, or pre-esthetic sense."[39] It is regrettable that Champigny did not develop this line of thought further, for it is somewhat difficult to determine precisely what he means in this case by "platonic," or even "esthetic." He does not see in this sense a "practical signal," but an esthetic sense. But let us reappraise the problem in terms of the function of language, the concept of the utilitarian, and the privileged position of man in relation to nature.

One might at first assume that the garden smiled because it was lying in wait, ready to burst out again at any time. But it is significant that it did not smile until Roquentin arrived at the gate, a point from which he could look back at a Nature subjugated, humanized by man's fence. Nature enclosed is Nature controlled. In *Baudelaire*, Sartre related an anecdote about a friend who was filling his glass from the kitchen water faucet. His brother said to him, "Tu ne veux pas plutôt de la *vraie* eau?" and went to get the water pitcher.

> La vraie eau c'était l'eau délimitée et comme repensée par son contenant transparent, et qui, du coup, perdant son air échevelé et toutes les souillures dont la chargeait sa promiscuité avec l'évier, participait à la pureté sphérique et transparente d'une oeuvre humaine; ce n'était pas l'eau folle, l'eau vague, l'eau suintante, stagnante ou ruis-selante, mais le métal ramassé au fond de la carafe, humanisé par son récipient.[40]

There is Roquentin's smiling garden: a circle is not being, nor is a square fence. This is perhaps what Champigny means by "platonic," but I would prefer the word "humanized."

And Roquentin sees a *regard* on the objects, the things in the park. "C'était là, sur le tronc du marronnier . . . c'était *le* marronier." (191) It is no longer a raw existent: Roquentin calls it a tree, a *marronnier*; the word is back, man's magic word is back, and the raw existent is again a tree, for *marronnier* means humanized object; Roquentin regains his privileged position by means of language.

At the gate Roquentin is perceiving the "véritable secret d'existence." And that secret seems to be that he had already seized on things "une sorte d'air complice." He does not know if that look is addressed to him, but "c'était là, dans l'attente, ça ressemblait à un regard." It is impossible, of course, not to recall now Baudelaire's

> La Nature est un temple où de vivants piliers
> Laissent parfois sortir de confuses paroles;
> L'Homme y passe à travers des forêts de symboles
> Qui l'observent avec des regards familiers.

This is apparently the same "regard familier" that Roquentin is getting here. Besides, he sees on things what appear to be "des pensées qui s'arrêtaient en route, qui s'oubliaient, qui oubliaient ce qu'elles avaient voulu penser et qui restaient comme ça, . . . avec un drôle de petit sens qui les dépassait." (191) In Part I we discussed Sartre's treatment of Baudelaire and his relation to the concept of *travail* which humanized raw nature, the *analyse bourgeoise*, and the anti-naturalist trend which developed by way of Marx and was adopted (according to Sartre) by

Baudelaire; thus he explained Baudelaire's fascination for the concept of *travail*, for changing Nature, and his intention in the production of poetry: Baudelaire wanted to produce artificiality and thus humanize Nature in his own way. Baudelaire, wrote Sartre, "a toujour été tenté par l'idée que les choses sont des pensées objectivées et comme solidifiées. Ainsi pouvait-il s'y mirer. Mais les réalités naturelles n'ont pour lui aucune signification. Elle ne veulent rien dire."[41] But the garden is, for Roquentin, no longer Nature: he considers it from the humanizing gate, and the incantation "marronnier" puts the tree in its place. We have see Lucien Fleurier try the same thing as he sat under the chestnut tree muttering, "Marronnier!" The tree did not react the way Mama did when he called her, but he named it nevertheless and threatened it: "Sale arbre, sale marronnier! attends voir, attends un peu! Et il lui donna des coups de pied."[42] Lucien will never have the nausea—he knows his rights and he knows what words are for.

What are we going to conclude from this scene? If we consider Sartre's subsequent career, I think we may take it as a statement of optimism: the external world may be menacing at times, but man, by technology, by language, need not founder in the "surrealist" world. Nausea still exists, but man is not destroyed by it; in fact, real life beings with nausea, or the other side of despair.

Conclusion

We will now draw together some generalizations about Sartre and the surrealists, by considering their answers to certain basic problems.

Where is the order that is perceived in the external world? The surrealist believes that it lies in man, and that, therefore, by surrealist activity that order may be broken down. If it actually existed in the external world, there would be no use in fighting against it (one would become like Captain Ahab in *Moby Dick*, pitting himself against an evil order in the universe: tragic, heroic, and futile). Thus the revolution in men's *minds* is a surrealist concern. Sartre also believed that order lies in man, but that he may impose it on the formless external world by language, technology, the *analyse bourgeoise*, etc. In fact, if order existed in the external world, from the Sartrean point of view there would be no absurdity.

Thus both see order as lying in man, versus a formless vision of the external world, of Nature. The options are either to break down the arbitrary and no longer valid existing order as is the case with the surrealists, or to impose a more lucid and efficacious order as is the case with Sartre; but both are essentially the same attitude toward man and things, except for the moral, prescriptive decision on the part of Sartre. He then shows some bitterness toward surrealist activity because he recognizes that their activity is possible, even effective to a certain extent. It is as if two men recognized the power of the atom, but one wanted to use it to destroy something he considered evil, and the other wanted to use it to build something he considered valuable.

Order for Roquentin lies in himself; as he reflects on his experiences, he remarks that he has tried vainly to think something on objects, "*sur eux.*" ". . . [E]t déjà j'avais senti leurs qualités, froides et inertes, se dérober, glisser entre mes doigts. Les bretelles d'Adolphe, l'autre soir, au "Rendez-Vous des Cheminots." Elles *n'étaient pas* violettes." (184) And

as for the root of the tree, "Ce noir, là, contre mon pied," it takes on all
the *corréspondances* of Baudelaire: it resembled

> une couleur mais aussi . . . à une meurtrissure ou encore à une sécrétion, à un suint
> . . . à une odeur . . . de terre mouillée, de bois tiède et mouillé, une odeur noire
> étendue comme un vernis sur ce bois nerveux, un saveur de fibre mâchée, sucrée
> . . . (185)

But that black is not on the root: "Je ne le *voyais* pas simplement ce noir:
la vue, c'est une invention abstraite, une idée nettoyée, simplifiée, une
idée d'homme." (185)

There is a great similarity between the absurdity of Sartre and that
of the surrealists, even if the surrealists did not develop it as a coherent
term in a unified vision of things. It arises from the confrontation of man
with the world, a confrontation that seems to promise no valid, lasting
results. From this state of affairs there is no salvation. There is no salvation in the world. "Chercher le réconfort dans une croyance me semble
vulgaire," wrote Breton. "Il est indigne de supposer un remède à la
souffrance morale."[1] From this basic absurdity both surrealism and Sartrean existentialism begin: their approaches are ways of dealing with it.

Consequently the concept of absurdity is intimately linked with the
menacing aspect of the "surrealist" world, that world of matter, that raw
material which is the subject matter of physics. But, even if the external
world, that brute nature without man, is threatening, and even if facticity,
man's connection with the *en-soi* exists, one still cannot accept the concept of absurdity on other than a metaphysical level—particularly if one
believes in the efficacy of the Marxist-utilitarian attitude toward the object, and the efficacious use of language to bring the world under man's
control.

On the socio-political level, Sartrean man has no logical justification
for the belief in absurdity: it is purely a metaphysical concept. Futility,
on the sociopolitical Marxist level, is nonexistent on account of the *analyse bourgeoise* and the magical function of language. This idea seems
to reflect Sartre's evolution from individual to social preoccupations. In
this sense, the surrealists (theoretically) remain in the realm of the formless unstable world, faced with absurdity and futility; Sartre opposed
them and went on to the Marxist world of social actions.

If man does not perceive order in the external world, if that order
comes from himself, it is inevitable that he is perceiving his own constructs or that he believes in magic. The surrealist preoccupation with the
occult and magic is not too different from Sartre's belief in the efficacy
of language, that one-to-one relationship of word and referent which al-

lows man to become master of an *en-soi* only insofar as the *pour-soi* is kept separate from it and does not founder in primitive nondifferentiation.

The location of this order accounts for Roquentin's original confusion about what was happening to him. Had he changed, or was it the world? "Je crois que c'est moi qui ai changé; c'est la solution la plus simple. La plus désagréable aussi." (14) Why should it be more disagreeable that he had changed than that the world was altering its character? Roquentin insists on retaining his intellectual integrity, even if the world outside begins to lose its coherence. He does not believe that he is insane, even during and after his most extreme experiences with nondifferentiation. He maintains his *pour-soi* intact.

The attitude toward the object that Roquentin finally ends up with, is that of a lucid *pour-soi*, who can relegate that object to its proper utilitarian role. It reflects Sartre's concern with condemning the *objet surréaliste* as we saw in *Littérature*. He is then prepared or at least predisposed to take his position as a manipulator of the external world, i.e., as a capitalist or a Marxist—both have the same attitude toward the object but differ as to who should benefit from its manipulation.

La Nausée thus offers us an intimation of Sartre's evolution toward a philosophy that *uses* objects, and in its condemnation of the bourgeoisie of Bouville, that batch of *salauds* who turns rights into things to be possessed, seems to turn Sartre's affections toward the working class (which, on the other hand, could possibly count as many *salauds* among its members as the bourgeoisie). As Sartre remarked in "Situation de l'écrivain en 1947," the French author may be classified by his posture in relation to the bourgeoisie; by opting in favor of the proletariat, he falls into place according to his own basis for classification. Any option against the bourgeoisie certainly makes Marxist social philosophy seem an attractive and effective means of action.

As we look back on the surrealist effort to unify opposites, we ask ourselves if they succeeded. Since the answer involves an intimate knowledge of their individual minds as well as our own assessment of their creations, the easiest answer is that they tried.

But it is not accurate to see the surrealists as trying to unify opposites and Sartre as trying to keep them totally separate. Roquentin did not try, it is true, but he nevertheless experienced unification in the park: "J'*étais* la racine du marronnier," he said. (186) It is more accurate to say that the surrealists attempted the unification of opposites as an end in itself and a utopic goal; Sartre-Roquentin, on the other hand, perceiving the unification in nausea (a necessary but painful experience) continued by his insistence on the ontological categories of the *en-soi* and *pour-soi* to maintain the integrity of the *pour-soi*, *without*, however, losing sight of nausea: Nausea becomes a permanent part of the individual, for "la nausée . . . c'est moi."

In a very rough way, then, the surrealists are comparable to the Hinayana Buddhists, and Sartre to the Mahayanists. The Hinayanist sought personal salvation in his enlightenment; when he found Nirvana, he stepped off the wheel of life and death and stayed off, safe in his unity with the One. The Mahayanist wants enlightenment; however, he is willing to sacrifice himself for others. "As a result of this difference, Nirvana, for the Mahayanist, loses its original meaning of extinction and simply designates the state of the enlightened being. Such a being continues to live in the world, where he works for the salvation of sentient beings."[2] He never loses his awareness of Nirvana, however, but he goes on to other things.

The surrealist attempted to unify opposites, thus destroying absurdity, and leading to a utopia; his technique was automatism, and closely related to the dream. Thus surrealism "degenerated" into an esthetic movement. Sartrean existentialism, on the other hand, by its ontological categories prevents the *pour-soi* from being submerged, and concentrates on living with the absurdity in a dignified and satisfactory manner. Thus, it "degenerated" into a sociopolitical activism.

And so, except for the different moral attitudes taken toward such problems and their varying success at solving them, we have seen Sartre and the surrealists meet on several common and interrelated grounds: absurdity; a concern with man's relation to objects; the efficacy of language; social action and contact with the proletariat; a view of an unstable and amorphous Nature; order as being a human attribute, not a characteristic of the universe; a rejection of essences and the noumenon; and the problem of individual realization versus the aspect of man as a social entity: common twentieth-century concerns, shared by twentieth-century men.

Notes

Introduction

1. SURREALISME, n.m. Automatisme psychique pur par lequel on se propose d'exprimer, soit verbalement, soit par écrit, soit de toute autre manière, le fonctionnement réel de la pensée. Dictée de la pensée, en l'absence de tout contrôle exercé par la raison, en dehors de toute préoccupation esthétique ou morale. *Premier manifeste du surréalisme*.

Part I

1. Jacques Bersani, Michel Autrand, Jacques Lecarme, and Bruno Vercier, *La Littérature en France depuis 1945* (Paris: Bordas, 1970), p. 174. This book contains a succinct and pertinent survey of the development of surrealism since World War II, pp. 145–74.

2. Jean-Paul Sartre, *L'Etre et le Néant* (Paris: Gallimard, 1949), p. 91.

3. *Ibid.*, p. 92.

4. Georges Bataille, "Le Surréalisme et sa différence avec l'existentialisme," *Critique*, no. 2, juillet 1946, p. 110.

5. Michel Contat and Michel Rybalka, *Les Ecrits de Sartre* (Chronologie, bibliographie commentée) (Paris: Gallimard, 1970), p. 69.

6. Louis Aragon, *Traité du style* (Paris: Gallimard, 1928), p. 90.

7. Jean-Paul Sartre, *Le Mur*. 44th edition (Paris: Gallimard, 1939), p. 163. Subsequent page references are indicated by numbers in parentheses in the text.

8. Maurice Nadeau, *Histoire du surréalisme* (Paris: Editions du Seuil, 1945), p. 77.

9. *Ibid.*, p. 240.

10. *Ibid.*, p. 81.

11. André Breton, *Les Manifestes du surréalisme, suivis de prolégomènes à un troisième manifeste du surréalisme ou non* (Paris: Sagittaire, 1946), p. 53.

12. Pictured in Marcel Jean, *Histoire de la peinture surréaliste* (Paris: Editions du Seuil, 1959), p. 284.

13. Jean-Paul Sartre, *Qu'est-ce que la littérature*. Collection Idées (Paris: Gallimard, 1948), p. 222. Hereafter referred to as *Littérature*.

14. Nadeau, *Histoire du surréalisme*, p. 156.

15. *Ibid.*, p. 36.

16. *Ibid.*, p. 81.

17. *Ibid.*

18. *Ibid.*, p. 157.

19. Sartre, *Littérature*, p. 167.

20. *Ibid.*, p. 168.

21. *Ibid.*, p. 224.

22. *Ibid.*, p. 226.

23. For a discussion of this technique see Jean-Paul Sartre, "M. François Mauriac et la liberté," *Situations I* (Paris: Gallimard, 1947); and Edith Kern, "Sartre," in *Existential Thought and Fictional Technique* (New Haven: Yale University Press, 1970).

24. Breton, *Les Manifestes du surréalisme*, p. 53.

25. *Ibid.*

26. André Breton, *Les Pas perdus* (Paris: Gallimard, 1924), p. 20.

27. *Ibid.*, p. 19.

28. *Ibid.*, p. 20.

29. Contat and Rybalka, *Les Ecrits de Sartre*, p. 70.

30. See Nadeau, *Histoire*, pp. 142–43.

31. Jean-Paul Sartre, *Réflexions sur la question juive* (Paris: Paul Morihien, ed., 1946), p. 20.

32. Francis Jeanson, *Sartre par lui-même* (Paris: Editions de Seuil, (1965), p. 4.

33. Jean-Paul Sartre, "L'Homme et les choses," *Situations* I (Paris: Gallimard, 1947), p. 249.

34. Breton, *Les Manifestes*, p. 52.

35. Henri Clouard, *Histoire de la littérature française*, 2 vol. (Paris: ed. Michel Albin, 1947), I, p. 85.

36. *Le Surréalisme au service de la révolution*, May 1933, no. 5, p. 28.

37. See Nadeau, p. 193.

38. Contat and Rybalka, *Les Ecrits de Sartre*, p. 70.

39. Breton, *Les Manifestes*, p. 9.

40. *Ibid.*, p. 8.

41. *Ibid.*, p. 9.

42. *Ibid.*

43. Nadeau, *Histoire*, p. 195.

44. *Ibid.*, p. 195.

45. Sartre, *Littérature*, p. 220.

46. André Breton, *Nadja*. Edition entièrement revue par l'auteur (Paris: Gallimard, 1964), pp. 157ff. ". . . il [Huysmans] m'est peut-être le moins étranger de mes amis." *Nadja*, p. 16.

47. *Ibid.*, pp. 157ff.

48. For the superior beauty of sick women see Joris-Karl Huysmans, *Les Croquis parisiens* (Paris: Librairie Plon, n.d.); James Laver, *The First Decadent* (New York: Citadel Press, 1955), chap. 3; and for the study of morbid aspects of Romanticism and the Decadence in general, Mario Praz, *The Romantic Agony* (Cleveland: World Publishing Co., 1951).

49. *Littérature*, p. 235.

50. Contat and Rybalka, *Les Ecrits de Sartre*, p. 70.

51. Nadeau, *Histoire*, p. 103.

52. Contat, *Les Ecrits de Sartre*, p. 70.

53. *Ibid.*

54. *Littérature*, pp. 220ff. All page references in this section are indicated by numbers in parentheses.

55. Jean-Paul Sartre, "Une Idée fondamentale de Husserl: L'Intentionnalité," *Situations I* (Paris: Gallimard, 1947), pp. 31ff.

56. Jean, *Histoire de la peinture surréaliste*, p. 36.

57. Breton, *Les Manifestes*, p. 62.

58. *Ibid.*

59. On the functions of mandalas, see Carl G. Jung, *Secret of the Golden Flower* (New York: Harcourt Brace and World, 1931), and Carl G. Jung and C. Kerenyi, *Essays on a Science of Mythology*, Harper Torchbooks (New York: Harper and Row, 1949), pp. 10ff.

60. See M. Carrouges, *André Breton: les données fondamentales du surréalisme* (Paris: Gallimard, 1950), chap. 2.

61. André Breton, "Des Tendances les plus récentes de la peinture surréaliste," *Minotaure*, no. 12–13, 1939, p. 31.

62. Nadeau, p. 234.

63. Contat, *Les Ecrits de Sartre*, p. 406.

64. See for example Jacques Maritain, *Creative Intuition in Art and Poetry*, Bollingen Series XXXVI, Pantheon Books (Washington, D. C.: Kingsport Press, 1953); and Louis Gardet, "Recherches sur la mystique naturelle," in *Jacques Maritain, son oeuvre philosophique* (Paris: Desclée de Brouwer, 1948).

65. Hans Richter, *Dada: art et anti-art* (Bruxelles, Editions de la Connaissance, 1965), last chapter.

66. Edwyn Robert Bevan, *Later Greek Religion* (London: J. M. Dent and Sons, 1927), p. 52.

67. Aragon, *Traité du style*, p. 85.

68. *Ibid.*, p. 87.

69. *Ibid.*, p. 91.

70. Nadeau, pp. 233–34.

71. *Ibid.*, p. 234.

72. Tout porte à croire qu'il existe un certain point de l'esprit d'où la vie et la mort, le réel et l'imaginare, le passé et le futur, le communicable et l'incommunicable, le haut et le bas, cessent d'être perçus contradictoirement. C'est en vain qu'on chercherait à l'activité surréaliste un autre mobile que l'espoir de la détermination de ce point. (*Second manifeste*).

73. André Gide, *Le Prométhée mal enchaîné* (Paris: Gallimard, 1925), p. 21.

74. Jean-Paul Sartre, *Les Mots* (Paris: Gallimard, 1963), p. 11.

75. Contat, *Les Ecrits de Sartre*, p. 418.

76. Bertrand Russell, *History of Western Philosophy*, 11th paperback printing (New York: Simon and Schuster, 1965), p. 785.

77. Jean-Paul Sartre, *Baudelaire* (Paris: Gallimard, 1947), p. 118).

78. *Ibid*.

79. *Ibid*., p. 119.

80. *Ibid*., p. 120.

81. Contat, *Les Ecrits de Sartre*, p. 418.

82. Sartre, *Baudelaire*, p. 125.

83. *Ibid*., p. 121.

84. *Ibid*., p. 122.

85. *Ibid*.

86. *Ibid*., p. 123.

87. *Ibid*., p. 125.

88. *Ibid*., p. 127.

89. Frederic Jameson, *The Origins of a Style* (New Haven: Yale University Press, 1961), p. 100.

90. *Ibid*., p. 249.

91. Contat, *Les Ecrits de Sartre*, p. 398. Sartre has defended his apparent relegation of art to an inferior position "en mettant l'accent sur le lecteur et non sur le langage et redéfinit les rapports du lecteur à l'oeuvre." Contat, p. 412, a propos of *Que peut la littérature*.

92. René Marill-Albérès, "Neo-Marxism and Criticism of Dialectical Reasoning," in Edith Kern, *Sartre: A Collection of Critical Essays*, Twentieth Century Views (Englewood Cliffs, N. J.: Prentice-Hall, 1965), p. 164.

93. *Ibid*.

94. Breton, *Les Manifestes*, pp. 61–62.

95. Contat, p. 339.

96. Roger Garaudy, *Perspectives de l'homme* (Paris: Presses Universitaires, 1961), p. 61.

97. *Ibid.*, p. 64.

98. See Francis Jeanson, *Le Problème morale et la pensée de Sartre* (Paris: Editions du Seuil, 1965), pp. 91–92.

99. Garaudy, *Perspectives*, p. 64.

100. *Ibid.*, p. 65.

101. *Ibid.*, p. 66.

Part II

1. Laurent LeSage, "Paul Valéry and Jean-Paul Sartre: A Confrontation," *Modern Language Quarterly*, Vol. 32, No. 2, June 1971, p. 190.

2. For a discussion of this term see Fung Yu-Lan, *History of Chinese Philosophy*, trans. Derk Bodde. 2 vol. (Princeton: Princeton University Press, 1952), II, pp. 331ff., and II, p. 360ff. There are other terms for the same thing: Tathagata-garba, Chen-ju, the pure-in-nature Dharmakaya, etc.

3. Carrouges, *André Breton*, p. 29.

4. Chang Chung-yuan, *Taoism and Creativity* (New York: Julian Press, 1963), p. 9.

5. *Ibid.*

6. *L'Etre et le Néant*, p. 132.

7. *Ibid.*

8. *Ibid.*, p. 133.

9. *Ibid.*

10. *Ibid.*

11. *Ibid.*, p. 134.

12. *Ibid.*, p. 368.

13. Breton, *Les Manifestes*, p. 10.

14. *Ibid.*, p. 35.

15. Marcel Jean, *Histoire de la peinture surréaliste*, p. 208.

16. *Les Manifestes*, p. 36.

17. *Ibid.*, p. 27.

18. Marcel Jean, *Histoire*, p. 192 (picture).

19. René Grousset, *The Rise and Splendor of the Chinese Empire*, trans. of *Histoire de la Chine* by A. Watson-Gandy and T. Gordon (London: G. Bles, 1952), p. 28.

20. Edith Kern, *Existential Thought and Fictional Technique* (New Haven: Yale University Press, 1970), p. 117.

21. Jean-Paul Sartre, *La Nausée* (Paris: Gallimard, 1938), p. 182. All page references in this section are indicated by numbers in parentheses in the text.

22. Kern, *Existential Thought and Fictional Technique*, p. 117.

23. *Ibid.*

24. *Ibid.*, p. 119.

25. *Ibid.*

26. Jean, *Histoire*, p. 67.

27. *Ibid.*, p. 67.

28. *Ibid.*, pp. 95–96 (picture).

29. Contat, p. 26.

30. Kenneth Douglas, "The Self-Inflicted Wound," in Edith Kern, *Sartre, A Collection of Critical Essays*. Twentieth Century Views (Englewood Cliffs, N. J.: Prentice-Hall, 1962), p. 41.

31. *Ibid.*

32. Carl G. Jung, *The Secret of the Golden Flower*, and commentary (New York: Harcourt, Brace and World, 1931), p. 85.

33. Douglas, "The Self-Inflicted Wound," p. 41.

34. *L'Etre et le Néant*, p. 365.

35. *Ibid.*, p. 366.

36. Kern, *Existential Thought*, etc., p. 117.

37. *Baudelaire*, p. 122.

38. Robert Champigny, *Stages on Sartre's Way* (Bloomington: Indiana University Press, 1959), p. 34.

39. *Ibid*.

40. *Baudelaire*, p. 121.

41. *Ibid*., p. 119.

42. *Le Mur*, p. 143.

Conclusion

1. Breton, *Les Pas perdus*, p. 8.

2. Fung Yu-Lan, *History of Chinese Philosophy*, II, p. 238.

Bibliography

Aragon, Louis. *Traité du style*. Paris: Gallimard, 1928.

Bataille, Georges. "Le Surréalisme at sa différence avec l'existentialisme," *Critique*, no. 2, juillet 1946, pp. 99–110.

Bersani, J., Autrand, M., Lecarme, J., and Vercier, B. *La Littérature en France depuis 1945*. Paris: Editions Bordas, 1970.

Bevan, Edwyn Robert. *Later Greek Religion*. London and Toronto: J. M. Dent and Sons Ltd. New York: E. P. Dutton and Co., 1927.

Breton, André and Eluard, Paul. *L'Immaculée Conception*. Paris: Seghers, 1961.

Breton, André. *Les Manifestes du surréalisme, suivis de prolégomènes à un troisième manifeste du surrealisme ou non*, etc. Paris: Le Sagittaire, 1946. (with magnifying glass).

_____. *Nadja*. Edition entièrement revue par l'auteur. Paris: Gallimard, 1964.

_____. *Les Pas perdus*. Paris: Gallimard, 1924.

_____. *Situation du surréalisme entre les deux guerres*. Paris: Editions de la revue Fontaine, 1945.

Carrouges, M. *André Breton et les données fondamentales du surréalisme*. Paris: Gallimard, 1950.

Champigny, Robert. *Stages on Sartre's Way*. Indiana University Press, Bloomington, 1959.

Chang Chung-yuan. *Taoism and Creativity*. New York: Julian Press, 1963.

Clouard, Henri. *Histoire de la littérature française*. 2 volumes. Paris: Editions Albin Michel, 1947.

Contat, Michel and Rybalka, Michel. *Les Ecrits de Sartre* (Chronologie, Bibliographie commentée) Paris: Gallimard, 1970.

Douglas, Kenneth. *A Critical Bibliography of Existentialism* (the Paris school) Yale French Studies, special monograph, no. 1, New Haven, 1950.

_____. "The Self-Inflicted Wound," in Edith Kern, *Sartre: A Collection of Critical Essays*. Twentieth Century View. Englewood Cliffs, N. Y.: Prentice-Hall, 1962.

Duthuit, Georges. "Sartre's Last Class." *Transition 48* 1 (1):7ff, 1948; 1(2):98ff, 1958; 1(3):47ff, 1948, 1(4):96ff, 1948.

Dutt, K. Guru. *Existentialism and Indian Thought*. New York, 1960.

Epictetus. *Discourses*. Translation of George Long. Philadelphia: Henry Altemus, n.d.

Fung Yu-Lan. *History of Chinese Philosophy*. 2 volumes. Translation by Derk Bodde. Princeton: Princeton University Press, 1952.

Garaudy, Roger. *Perspectives de l'homme*. Paris: Presses Universitaires de France, 1961.

Gardet, Louis. "Recherches sur la mystique naturelle," in *Jacques Maritain, son oeuvre philosophique*. Paris: Desclée de Brouwer, 1948. (Further bibliography on this subject in Maritain, *Creative Intuition in Art and Poetry*, p. 93 n.)

Gide, André. *Les Caves du Vatican*. Paris: Nouvelle Revue française, 1922.

————. *Le Prométhée mal enchaîné*. Paris: Gallimard, 1925.

Grousset, René. *Rise and Splendor of the Chinese Empire*. Translation of *Histoire de la Chine* by A. Watson-Gandy and T. Gordon. London: G. Bles, 1952.

Huysmans, J.-K. *Croquis parisiens*. Paris: Librairie Plon, n.d.

Jameson, Frederic. *Sartre, The Origins of a Style*. New Haven and London: Yale University Press, 1961.

Jean, Marcel. *Histoire de la peinture surréaliste*. Editions du Seuil, Paris, 1959.

Jeanson, Francis. *Le Problème moral et la pensée de Sartre*. Editions du Seuil, Paris, 1955.

————. *Sartre par lui-même*. Paris: Editions du Seuil, 1955.

Jung, Carl G. and C. Kerenyi. *Essays on a Science of Mythology*. Harper Torchbooks, trans. R.F.D. Hull. New York: Harper and Row, 1963.

Jung, C. G. and Wilhelm, Richard. *The Secret of the Golden Flower*, and commentary. New York: Harcourt Brace and World, 1931.

Kern, Edith, *Existential Thought and Fictional Technique*. New Haven and London: Yale University Press, 1970.

————. *Sartre, a Collection of Critical Essays*. Twentieth-century views. Englewood Cliffs, N. J.: Prentice-Hall, 1962.

Laver, James. *The First Decadent*. (Being the Strange Life of J.-K. Huysmans) New York: Citadel Press, 1955.

LeSage, Laurent. "Paul Valéry and Jean-Paul Sartre—A Confrontation," *Modern Language Quarterly*. Vol. 32, no. 2, June 1971, pp. 189–205.

Maritain, Jacques. *Creative Intuition in Art and Poetry*. Bollingen Series XXXVI, Pantheon Books. Tennessee: Kingports Press. Copyright by trustees of National Gallery of Art, Washington, D. C., 1953.

Minotaure. Numbers 1–13. Arno Series of Contemporary Art No. 1. Authorized reprint. New York: Arno Press, 1968.

Nadeau, Maurice. *Histoire du surréalisme*. (Vol. 2. *Documents surréalistes*) Paris: Editions du Seuil, 1945.

Northrop, F. C. "The Undifferentiated Aesthetic Continuum," *Philosophy East and West*. April 1964.

Praz, Mario. *The Romantic Agony*. Cleveland: World Publishing Co., 1951.

La Révolution surréaliste. Numbers 1–12. Arno Series of Contemporary Art. New York: Arno Press, n.d.

Richter, Hans. *Dada: art et anti-art*. Bruxelles: Editions de la Connaissance, 1965.

Russell, Bertrand. *History of Western Philosophy*. 11th paperback printing. New York: Simon and Schuster, 1965.

Sade marquis de. *Les 120 Journées de Sodome*. Vol. XIII of Oeuvres complètes. Paris: Cercle du livre précieux, 1964.

Sartre, Jean-Paul. *Baudelaire*. Paris: Gallimard, 1947.

————. *Critique de la Raison dialectique*. Paris: Gallimard, 1960.

————. *L'Etre et le Néant*. Paris: Gallimard, 1949. Translated as *Being and Nothingness*, Hazel Barnes, Philosophical Library, New York, 1956.

————. "Une Idée fondamentale de Husserl." *Situations* I. Paris: Gallimard, 1947.

————. "M. François Mauriac et la liberté," *Situations* I. Paris: Gallimard, 1947.

————. *La Mort dans l'âme*. Paris: Gallimard, 1949.

————. *Les Mots*. Paris: Gallimard, 1963.

————. *Le Mur*. 44th edition. Paris: Gallimard, 1939.

————. *La Nausée*. Paris: Gallimard, 1938.

————. *Qu'est-ce que la littérature?* Collection idées. Paris: Gallimard, 1948.

————. *Réflexions sur la question juive*. Paris: Paul Morihien éditeurs, 1946.

_____. *Saint Genêt, comédien et martyr*. Paris: Gallimard, 1952.

_____. *Le Sursis*. Paris: Gallimard, 1945.

Le Surréalisme au service de la révolution. Numbers 1–6. Arno Press, authorized reprint, Series of Contemporary Art, no. 4, New York, 1968.

Teilhard de Chardin, Pierre. *Le Phénomène humain*. Paris: Editions du Seuil, 1955.

Index